Advocate Collection

THE ADVOCATE COLLECTION

Vegetarians in the Fast Lane

D0861417

"*Vegetarians in the Fast Lane* gives excellent directions to us all—vegetarians and nonvegetarians. Whether used twice a week or daily, all can benefit from this book, which is designed to help us, who are of necessity time conscious, improve our nutritional status. I find the recipes nutritionally sound, while needing a minimum of both supermarket-searching time and kitchen-preparation time. What a *great* idea! More than a cookbook, *Vegetarians in the Fast Lane* serves as a nutritional guide to better health. *Get this book,* and more importantly, *use this book* regularly. Get regular exercise and take the time to enjoy your family and friends. When you get to your golden years, you'll reflect and say, "I only wish I had done it sooner."

Ripley Hollister, M.D.
American Board of Family Practice, Diplomat
American Academy of Family Physicians, Fellow

"An excellent book . . . For those who enjoy cooking and healthier meals, these recipes certainly are fulfilling to the palate. 'Veggies' are not merely steamed vegetables. Travis and Carla have proved this. So try some of these delicious foods using these recipes. You will absolutely crave more."

B. C. Patel, M.D.
Gastroenterology, Liver Diseases

"*Vegetarians in the Fast Lane* tells you what to do and how to do it. There are grains with strange names. They taste better than the ones you know. One powered the Aztecs. A nearby store sells it now or will after you talk to the manager."

Bill Calkins
Former Seventh-Day Adventist pastor, now a
vegetarian cooking class instructor (among other things)

THE ADVOCATE COLLECTION

Vegetarians in the
FAST LANE

Carla L. Henry and Travis J. Henry

Illustrated by Lisa Silva Pate

*

641.563
H521v

PELICAN PUBLISHING COMPANY
Gretna 1996

East Baton Rouge Parish Library
Baton Rouge, Louisiana

Copyright © 1996
By Carla L. Henry and Travis J. Henry

Illustrations copyright © 1996
By Lisa Silva Pate
All rights reserved

The word "Pelican" and the depiction of a pelican are
trademarks of Pelican Publishing Company, Inc., and are
registered in the U.S. Patent and Trademark Office.

Library of Congress Cataloging-in-Publication Data

Henry, Carla L.
    Vegetarians in the fast lane / by Carla L. Henry and Travis J.
Henry ; illustrated by Lisa Silva Pate.
       p. cm.
    Includes index.
    ISBN 1-56554-135-9 (pbk.)
    1. Vegetarian cookery. 2. Quick and easy cookery. I. Henry,
    Travis J. II. Title.
TX837.H46 1996
641.5'636—dc20
                                       96-18882
                                          CIP

Manufactured in the United States of America

Published by Pelican Publishing Company, Inc.
1101 Monroe Street, Gretna, Louisiana 70053

We dedicate this book to Roger Bresnan, Carla's brother and Travis's uncle and godfather. Roger introduced us to his vegetarian dishes many years ago when a vegetarian diet and life-style seemed so alien. Our love and thanks for all the special moments you gave and continue to give us.

CARLA L. HENRY
TRAVIS J. HENRY

Special thanks to Yolanda Fintor, friend and coauthor of our cookbook, Souper Skinny Soups. I'm so grateful you and I happened to meet in Joan Jones's creative writing class at Pierce College more than ten years ago. What a wonderful journey we are sharing!

CARLA L. HENRY

To Michael and Neil, my two sons, who provide me with all the happiness and inspiration a father can want.

TRAVIS J. HENRY

Contents

Preface

FROM THE AUTHOR, THE MOM

Although I have always been health conscious—especially in my role as a mother raising three children, Travis, Zachary, and Justine—I did not consider the merits of a vegetarian diet. When Travis converted to his vegetarian diet, I was surprised but relieved. I had noticed during and after his enlistment in the U.S. Army, he consumed a much higher intake of red meat. With a diet too marbled in cholesterol-rich steak, he then pursued a career in management, which included long hours and high stress. Early on in this field, he experienced a heart arrhythmia. So his conversion to a vegetarian diet was quite a relief to me.

Travis began experimenting and compiling his own vegetarian recipes. He then called me and said, "Mom, since you know how to write a cookbook,* maybe you could help me write a vegetarian cookbook for people with busy lives." I said, "Great idea, we'll combine our recipes and knowledge to coauthor this cookbook."

I have found coauthoring with my son very rewarding, I have learned even more about nutrition and have the joy of spending more time (via phone calls and visits) together with Travis. I believe the delicious recipes and time management information in *Vegetarians in the Fast Lane* will help all types of vegetarians and occasional meat eaters enjoy the health benefits of a well-balanced diet.

*I coauthored with my friend Yolanda Fintor *Souper Skinny Soups,* published by Pelican Publishing Company and released in October 1993.

FROM THE AUTHOR, THE SON

Being a vegetarian has proven to be a much healthier way of life. Vegetarians who diet properly lead healthier and longer lives with fewer health problems than people who consume meat. According to my research, up to 60 percent of all deaths in the United States are diet related, costing Americans over 110 billion dollars a year in direct healthcare expenditures. I knew I didn't want to become a part of those statistics.

Up until now most people who consider becoming vegetarians have hesitated because of time constraints. Even the beef industry has launched a mass advertising campaign—"Beef. It's What's For Dinner.®"—targeting all of America with our busy schedules.

I found that most vegetarian cookbooks are time consuming and impractical for today's vegetarian. Maintaining a healthy vegetarian diet with meal preparation under 30 minutes was my goal. *Vegetarians in the Fast Lane* is more than a cookbook, it is also a guide to better health. This cookbook will allow you to maintain a healthier way of life without having to invest in any more food preparation time than you're probably already spending. When I had two jobs, I used cookbooks with very time-consuming recipes. So, like a lot of people who have busy schedules, I gave up on eating nutritious meals. I felt sluggish and lacked energy; I knew I was eating poorly. To get back on track, I began planning better meals.

Coming from a family of chefs and good cooks, I decided to write a book that I could use to maintain a healthy diet easily. Thanks to the support of family and good friends, my mother and I present to you a practical cookbook for a healthier way of life. *Vegetarians in the Fast Lane* will enable you to maintain a healthy diet around your busy schedule.

What Is a Vegetarian?

If asked what a vegetarian is, most people reply, "Someone who doesn't eat meat." But, because every individual is unique with different needs and values, there are many types and considerations to being a vegetarian.

Some people go through phases in their life, become vegetarians, and then revert back to an omnivorous diet because it seemed easier to be a meat eater. Others read about nutritional issues such as the drug and hormonal injecting of animals for reasons like "fattening" or increasing milk production, and they become alarmed. People with health issues (coronary heart disease, stroke, cancer, obesity, etc.) often convert to the healthier vegetarian diet. And others adopt a philosophical or religious objection to eating meat.

Vegetarians in the Fast Lane is a cookbook for all types of vegetarians, even meat eaters, who want to enjoy the many tantalizing recipes from around the world that can be prepared without spending hours in the kitchen. Even occasional vegetarians will want to live vicariously in exotic lands and awaken their taste buds to previously unexplored flavors. There is an extra bonus, too, in adopting a vegetarian diet—a healthier you!

TYPES OF VEGETARIANS

A **vegan** abstains from all animal-origin foods, including meat, fowl, fish, eggs, and dairy products.

A **macrobiotic** eats grains, fresh vegetables, beans, and sea vegetables with a concern for food preparation and proportion. The macrobiotic diet is concerned, philosophically, with food as a form of packaging the energy (*ki*) that sustains life. A follower of a macrobiotic diet is concerned with achieving a balance in terms of the Oriental philosophy of yin and yang in food preparation and intake with regulation of the flow of *ki*. Yin (feminine) foods grow rapidly and are expansive, such as fruits. Yang (masculine) foods grow more slowly in colder climates, such as root crops (potatoes, turnips, and carrots). The macrobiotic diet is controversial because it is high in sodium and there is a high volume of cooked grain. Initial adjustments to achieve the balance of yin and yang in food preparation may be prohibitive to an active lifestyle.

A **lacto-vegetarian** adds dairy products to his vegan diet.

An **lacto-ovo-vegetarian** adds dairy products and eggs to the vegan diet. This diet is recommended for growing children on a vegetarian diet.

A **pesco-vegetarian** includes dairy products, eggs, and fish in the vegan diet.

A **semi-vegetarian** eats dairy products, eggs, fish, and occasionally, poultry.

SOURCES OF NECESSARY VITAMINS AND MINERALS

Abstinence from all animal-origin foods can lead to vitamin and mineral deficiencies if the diet is not monitored carefully. But awareness and planning can allow the vegan or macrobiotic to obtain more of these important vitamins and minerals.

Calcium: Green leafy vegetables such as spinach and kale, and blackstrap molasses

Iron: Blackstrap molasses, cherry juice, green leafy vegetables, and dried fruits

Copper: Nuts, legumes, molasses, and raisins

Manganese: Whole grains, green leafy vegetables, legumes, nuts, and pineapples

Vitamin B12: Vitamin B12 supplements and fortified soy milk (check the label to be certain the supplement contains at least 3 or 4 mcg. of vitamin B12, listing cobalamin as a source), cereal, textured vegetable protein (TVP®), and yeast, such as Red Star® brand T-6635+ nutritional yeast

Zinc: Nuts, pumpkin and sunflower seeds, molasses, mushrooms, wheat bran and wheat germ, and brewer's yeast

A lower incidence of chronic diseases and a longer life span are attributed to a vegetarian diet. However, many dietitians and nutritionists report that vegans and macrobiotics should supplement their diets with nutrients such as calcium, iron, copper, zinc, manganese, and Vitamin B12.

RECOMMENDED DAILY CONSUMPTION

A vegan diet should consume the following daily nutrients:

- 3 to 5 servings of vegetables combining raw and cooked such as carrots, broccoli, cauliflower, cabbage, green beans, potatoes, and spinach, etc. (A serving counts as ½ cup [115 gm.] of a cooked vegetable or 1 cup [225 gm.] of raw, leafy greens.)

- 2 to 4 servings of fruit, combining fresh fruit such as bananas and apples, fruit juice, and dried fruits. (A serving counts as 1 medium-size fruit such as an apple, ½ cup [115 gm.] of sliced fruit, or ¾ cup [180 ml.] of fruit juice.)

- 3 or 4 servings of legumes such as lentils or kidney or garbanzo beans. (A serving counts as ½ cup [115 gm.] of cooked legumes.)

- 1 to 2 servings of nuts and seeds such as walnuts, almonds, and sunflower, sesame, and pumpkin seeds. (A serving counts as ¾ cup [170 gm.] of whole nuts, ½ cup [115 gm.] of pine nuts, or ½ cup [115 gm.] of seeds.)

- 2 servings of soybean-based products such as tofu and soy milk. (A serving counts as 4 oz. [115 gm.] of tofu or [125 ml.] soy milk.)

- 6 or more servings of whole grains or staples such as cereal, whole-wheat bread, rice, bulgur, and pasta. (A serving counts as ½ cup [115 gm.] of cooked grains, cereal, rice, or pasta; 1 slice of bread; or half of a bagel.)

- A small amount of unsaturated fats such as canola or olive oil used in cooking.

Just a few modifications to a diet can have multiple benefits, a healthier body with reduced susceptibility to diseases, improved weight maintenance, and even a financial savings, both short and long term. Reducing or eliminating meat in a diet saves money at the checkout stand and costly doctor and hospital treatments.

Being a vegetarian is easy! Buy an assortment of fresh and dried fruits to grab as you leave the house. Many supermarkets have packaged raw vegetables ready to eat or use in recipes. Buy fruit juice instead of soda. The microwave is a real boon to vegetarians; vegetables can be prepared in minutes. For instance, a sweet potato can be pierced with a fork, placed on a microwave grill or towel, and cooked in less than 10 minutes. Add a bowl of a leftover staple reheated in the final 2 to 3 minutes, and a quick, healthy meal is ready to eat.

Many natural food stores carry staples in bulk. For new vegetarians, it seems too involved to learn how to cook staples. Understanding the value of staples and having a good reference on preparing staples were of great importance in writing *Vegetarians in the Fast Lane.* Rule 1: Always cook extra so there are leftovers. Rule 2: Experiment with all the different staples. We prefer different staples; for Travis it is couscous, for Carla it is bulgur. Others might enjoy millet or rice, or any or all of the choices. Staples are the base for many of the recipes, so experiment and enjoy!

CHAPTER 1
Time Management
Applied to Food Preparation

Preparing flavorful, nutritious meals that can be prepared in minutes is a concern for almost everyone. Vegetarian diets are often less costly than nonvegetarian diets. However, there "seems" to be more preparation time involved and less opportunity to take advantage of drive-through fast-food restaurants. The following are suggestions on maintaining a vegetarian diet, or any diet, in which time constraints are an issue.

USE OF COOKING UTENSILS AND TOOLS

Blender. Necessary for processing ingredients for many recipes and preparing the protein drinks and liquid beverages.

Can opener. The real world doesn't always allow the luxury of growing vegetables in a backyard garden for optimum fresh and natural food consumption. Also, many times a hectic schedule doesn't permit cooking from scratch. A hand-operated can opener doesn't waste electricity, doesn't break down, and doesn't need kitchen-counter space.

Cast-iron skillet. A cast-iron skillet emits iron deposits in food while cooking. The added iron is especially beneficial for women, who have higher iron requirements than men. To properly care for a cast-iron skillet, wash with very little soap and rinse immediately, leaving a small amount of water in the skillet. Then heat over medium-high heat until the water evaporates. Add 2 tbsp. (30 ml.) of canola oil and spread evenly with paper towel.

Cordless phone. No, it's not a cooking utensil, but it allows the freedom to take care of phone calls while spending time in the kitchen. Not recommended for novice cooks who need to concentrate when preparing food.

Crock pot or slow cooker. A crock pot is convenient because food can cook while the cook is gone. There's less mess, no food splattering on the walls, and only one pot to clean. In preparing soups, cook on "low" 6 to 8 hours, then turn the setting up to "high" and add the pastas and rices in the last 30 to 60 minutes.

Food processor. A great tool to speed up chopping vegetables and processing ingredients.

Knife. Invest in a good quality serrated vegetable knife that doesn't require sharpening. A good quality knife will save slicing time and is less hazardous to use. While attempting to cut through a hard vegetable, a dull knife will roll off the surface, which makes finger cuts more probable.

Microwave oven. The microwave does an excellent job of cooking vegetables in minutes and reheating refrigerated or frozen foods. Follow the microwave manufacturer's cooking instructions for heating time. A few rules: Loosely cover foods so steam can escape using wax paper, plastic wrap, or a container lid left partially opened; pierce unpeeled vegetables such as potatoes, yams, or apples with a fork; let vegetables or fruits stand 3 to 5 minutes after microwaving before serving.

Teflon stirring utensils. Use a long-handled Teflon-coated spoon and fork to protect the finish of nonstick pans.

Vegetable brush. It is faster to use than a vegetable peeler is and preserves the healthy vitamins in the vegetable skin.

Wok. Essential for vegetarians because of the stir-fry vegetable and tofu dishes they prepare. Also, the wok reduces oil-splattering cleanup.

SHOPPING

Make a list. There's nothing more frustrating than to be in the middle of preparing a recipe and realize there's a missing ingredient. Checking off items from a list that is organized according to your grocer's arrangement of products is a quick and efficient way to ensure that items aren't forgotten or overlooked.

Shopping schedule. Shopping time can be reduced by as much as 30 minutes if peak shopping hours are avoided. *Do not* shop on Saturday. *Do not* shop right after work if your workday ends at 5 P.M. *Do* shop at natural food stores for fresh organic fruits and vegetables—usually the shopping time is shorter than at major supermarket chains. *Do* shop bimonthly or monthly for nonperishable items at supermarkets.

FOOD PREPARATION

Vegetables. Vegetables should be cleaned, chopped, and then stored in the refrigerator immediately after returning from a shopping trip. This greatly reduces recipe preparation time. It's also a good time to actually prepare a few recipes to refrigerate or freeze for later use. Many of the recipes you plan to prepare for the week already have the vegetables and other ingredients in those shopping bags. This is an opportunity to prepare meals before putting away the necessary ingredients.

Cooking time. Many people who work find that cooking several recipes at one time frees them up for other events during a hectic schedule. As suggested above, shopping and cooking time combined can greatly reduce food preparation efforts. Learning how to coordinate food preparation steps is essential. For instance, while the water for pasta is being heated, the sauce can be prepared. In between stirring the pasta after adding to the boiling water, the garlic bread or salad can be prepared.

Crock-pot cooking. Crock-pot cooking is beneficial in both time management and the retention of vitamins and minerals. It's a joy to know that, when the cook comes home, the meal is ready to serve. If morning time is limited, chop the vegetables the prior evening, store in the refrigerator, and add to the crock pot in the morning. In the morning it only takes a few minutes to place all the recipe ingredients into the crock pot and turn the crock pot on. Upon returning home from work, the meal (casserole, beans, marinara sauce, or soup) is done and ready to eat. For use with beans, soak the beans overnight in the crock pot. The next morning, drain and return the beans to the crock pot and add the vegetables and spices. Crock-pot cooking also reduces cleanup of wall splatters because the lid is on, and there is only one pot to clean!

Cleanup. Clean as you cook. Fill the sink with hot water and a squirt of dish detergent. Put the ingredients away after using them and wipe up the cooking work space. After using the cooking utensils and pots and pans, place them in hot sudsy water to soak or wash. Don't allow food to dry on the utensils or pans; it takes triple effort to scrub off later. This keeps the kitchen clean and orderly in a time-saving way. Keeping the counters, cutting boards, and cooking utensils clean immediately after using also protects against possible food bacteria buildup. Use an antibacterial cleanser or diluted bleach to keep kitchens uncontaminated.

CHAPTER 2
Food Storage Tips

To be able to eat nutritional meals while leading a very active life-style, it's important that food be stored properly. The following are important storage tips for certain foods:

Avocados should be stored in a brown bag at room temperature for a few days. An avocado will brown immediately after peeling or cutting. Rub lime or lemon juice on the exposed fruit, then wrap in plastic wrap and store in the refrigerator for up to 8 hours.

Bagels should be stored in an airtight plastic bag for overnight. If needed to be kept for 2 or 3 days, store in an airtight plastic bag in the refrigerator. To store for longer periods, doublewrap in plastic and place in the freezer. Bagels can be easily warmed in the microwave, toaster, or broiler oven.

Keep **bread** stored either in a special bread box or a cool, dry place. Bread can be kept frozen for several months; doublewrap in plastic to keep out other food odors. It is best to freeze the portion of the bread loaf that will not be used within a few days to prevent mold and to prevent the loaf from getting hard.

Cheese should be kept tightly wrapped in its original wrapper or in plastic wrap for up to two weeks in the refrigerator.

Eggs should be stored in their original carton in the back of the refrigerator. They can be kept for up to two weeks in the refrigerator.

Flour contains minute insect eggs invisible to the human eye. It is best stored in the refrigerator to prevent the eggs from hatching. Another recommendation is to place bay leaves in cupboards near the flour and staples to prevent an insect infestation.

Frozen foods must be kept frozen. Place the frozen foods in the freezer immediately after returning home from the grocery store. If they thaw, bacteria breeds rapidly and the frozen food becomes hazardous to your health.

Fruits should not be stored in plastic bags, but in brown bags in a cool, dry place or in the vegetable tray inside the refrigerator.

Garlic and **onions** can be stored in the open air for up to one month. Garlic can also be stored in oil for long periods of time. Peel the garlic and break the buds apart. Place the garlic in a jar and cover the garlic completely with oil. Seal with a tight-fitting lid and store in a cool, dry place.

Herbs and **spices** are aromatic and lose their potency the longer they stay in jars; buy smaller quantities in natural food stores and immediately seal in small containers with tight-fitting lids. Store in cool, dry places. *Do not store in spice racks on kitchen walls.* If properly stored, herbs will retain flavor up to several months, spices up to six months.

Legumes should be kept in tightly covered containers in a cool, dry place.

Mayonnaise should be refrigerated immediately after opening. It will keep in the refrigerator for up to three months. Do not freeze mayonnaise. Sandwiches, salads, etc. prepared with mayonnaise can spoil easily. Keep in the refrigerator or a cooler until ready to serve.

Unopened **mushrooms** should be stored in the original package; once opened, store in a paper bag for 5 to 7 days. Clean just before using.

Nuts in the shell can be stored for months in a cool, dry place. Shelled nuts should be kept in sealed plastic bags in the freezer. Frozen walnuts keep well for a whole year and defrost in minutes for fast meal preparation. Pecans stay fresh in the refrigerator up to 9 months; frozen, up to 2 years. For a week's supply of shelled nuts, keep in an airtight jar in the refrigerator.

Bottled **oil** will keep well at room temperature for several months. Oil should not be refrigerated; it will congeal, making it impossible to use. However, if you live in an extremely hot climate, oil should be purchased in smaller containers and used within three to four weeks to avoid becoming rancid.

Dry **pasta** can be stored in a cool, dry place up to a year after purchase. Whole-grain pasta should be stored in the refrigerator to avoid becoming rancid. Fresh pasta must be kept refrigerated. Cooked pasta should be rinsed with cold water, placed in a stainless steel bowl, covered with water, and stored in the refrigerator for up to 3 days.

Fresh **salad greens** should be put unwashed in a plastic bag and stored in the refrigerator. Wash and dry before using.

Fresh **tofu** should be refrigerated immediately after purchase. The tofu water should be changed every two days to avoid bacteria buildup. Tofu will keep one week if properly stored. Frozen tofu can be kept in the same container purchased from the store. After storing in the freezer for one week, the texture changes from soft to spongy. The frozen tofu should then be removed from the freezer, thawed at room temperature, drained of all liquid, and squeezed dry. Then crumble or slice for use in a recipe. Do not leave out to thaw at room temperature for more than 6 hours.

Fresh **vegetables** should be cooked within 8 hours for maximum nutritional value. Supermarkets now have available packaged fresh vegetables that are precut, cleaned, and ready to use. However, if fresh vegetables are not eaten almost immediately, it is actually more nutritious to buy frozen vegetables. And, using frozen vegetables in recipes is less time-consuming; they are already cleaned, cut, and chopped.

FOOD AND NUTRITION SUBSTITUTES

Cashew nut milk. Cashews offer a high level of vitamin E and are a source of protein, unsaturated fats, B-complex vitamins, calcium, and several minerals. Cashew Nut Milk is an alternative to cow's milk for cooking or is a delicious drink on its own. The recipe is in chapter 4, "Breakfast."

Cow's milk. Use soy or coconut milk. Rice milk can be used as a substitute for cow's milk for drinking or adding to cereal. However, rice milk is often too thin to use in many recipes. Soy milk is rich in iron, thiamine, and niacin, but lacks the calcium and phosphorus of cow's milk. Rich sources of calcium are found in blackstrap molasses, green leafy vegetables, dried figs, legumes, nuts, and nori seaweed. *Note:* Seaweed is not recommended for low-sodium diets.

Egg. Use ¼ cup (60 ml.) egg beaters® egg substitute for one egg.

Fresh herbs. Dried herbs are easier to keep on hand and store. The basic guideline for substituting a dried herb for fresh is to use a ½ tsp. (2 gm.) of a dried herb for 2 tsp. (8 gm.) of a freshly minced herb. The equation is different for dried minced onion and parsley/cilantro flakes, 1 tsp. (4 gm.) dry to every 4 tsp. (16 gm.) of the fresh.

Garlic cloves. Use prepared minced garlic available in grocery stores; store in the refrigerator after opening.

Ghee (clarified butter). It's high in healthy monounsaturates, does not burn at high temperatures, and is a very flavorful substitute for butter or margarine. Ghee can be found in Indian markets or natural food stores.

Gingerroot. Fresh gingerroot does add the most flavor to a recipe, but keeping prepared minced gingerroot in the refrigerator can speed up food preparation. Natural food stores like Trader Joe's stocks prepared minced gingerroot. Ground ginger can also be mixed with a small amount of soy sauce for recipes calling for fresh gingerroot. The ratio is 1 tbsp. (15 ml.) to ¼ tsp. (1 gm.) ground ginger.

Margarine. Canola margarine is the healthiest choice for margarine as a substitute for butter. Many nutritionists recommend canola margarine, canola oil, and olive oil as the cooking fats to be used in food preparation.

Meat. Nuts, seeds, soybean, tofu, TVP®, and whole wheat can be added and combined to recipes to replace meat for texture and nutrients.

Omega-3 fatty acid. Oil in fish has an abundance of Omega-3 fatty acid. Alternative sources of Omega-3 for vegetarians can be found in canola oil, flaxseed oil, soybean products, and walnuts. Omega-3 is beneficial for helping to prevent heart attacks, stroke, and cancer.

Soy sauce. Lower sodium alternatives for soy sauce are found in tamari, a soybean derivative, and shoyu, a wheat derivative.

White sugar. In recipes, in place of 1 cup (225 gm.) of white sugar, substitute ½ cup (115 gm.) honey or molasses and reduce the total amount of other liquid ingredients by ¼ cup (60 ml.).

Worcestershire sauce. If vegetarian Worcestershire sauce is desired but not available in your area, substitute with A.1.® Steak Sauce.

CHAPTER 3
Staples

Staples are an important part of a vegetarian's diet. Hearty grains, such as bulgur and millet, offer a complex carbohydrate with high doses of vitamins and proteins. Meals prepared with staples help satisfy the appetite and are considered beneficial for weight maintenance. Individuals concerned with weight maintenance will want to reduce their intake of carbohydrates such as pasta and white rice, and replace those starches with the complex carbohydrates found in hearty grains and vegetables.

COUSCOUS

Couscous, a staple food for North Africans, is loaded with amino acids, minerals, and vitamins. Preparation and cooking time combined is under 10 minutes. This is a versatile staple that can be served hot or cold as a main dish; for breakfast; in salads; in snacks; or as a substitute for rice, pasta, or potatoes.

CONVENTIONAL COOKING

1 cup (250 ml.) water
1 tbsp. (15 gm.) butter
½ tsp. (2 gm.) salt
1 cup (225 gm.) couscous

In a saucepan, add water, butter, and salt; bring to a boil. Pour in couscous, stirring well. Turn off heat, cover, and let stand for 5 minutes. Fluff with a fork. Serves 4 or 5.

MICROWAVE COOKING

Combine the above ingredients in a microwave-safe dish. Stir together well and microwave on high power for 3½ minutes. Fluff with a fork. Serves 4 or 5.

KASHA

*Kasha, a Russian word for buckwheat,
is a derivative of the rhubarb plant.*

1 cup (225 gm.) kasha
1 egg, beaten
½ cup (115 gm.) carrot, grated
½ onion, chopped
1 cup (225 gm.) mushrooms, sliced
½ tsp. (2 gm.) tarragon
½ tsp. (2 gm.) salt
¼ tsp. (1 gm.) pepper
2 tbsp. (30 ml.) canola oil
2 cups (500 ml.) vegetable stock

In a small bowl, stir the kasha and egg together. Set aside.

Sauté the vegetables and spices in the canola oil in a heavy skillet for 5-6 minutes. Add the kasha-egg mixture and chop with a fork, stirring and cooking for about 2 minutes. Add the vegetable stock and bring to a boil. Cover with a tightly sealed lid, lower the heat, and simmer for about 15 minutes. Serves 4.

Tip: Use cooked kasha to stuff peppers or substitute for other rice dishes. Or mix with steamed vegetables and serve over cooked buttered egg noodles.

Hint: Available in natural food stores is a packaged product called Kashi. Kashi has seven whole grains, including kasha, and sesame; it can be prepared for breakfast, lunch, or dinner. Add fruit, nuts, yogurt, or different spices for variety. And like other staples, kashi can be included in stir-frys, salads, casseroles, or soups.

MILLET

Millet dates back to Stone-Age civilizations in Asia and Europe. It is a rich grain staple with more protein and iron, but fewer calories than rice.

1 cup (225 gm.) millet
3½ cups (875 ml.) water*

In a large saucepan, add millet and water. On medium-high heat, bring water to a boil. Lower heat, cover, and cook about 30 minutes. Serves 2.
*Substitute vegetable broth for a richer flavor and more vitamins.

Hint: Sauté the millet in a small amount of canola oil before adding the water for a "nutty" flavor.

QUINOA
(pronounced kē'nōə)

A hearty grain originally grown in the high Andes of South America. Quinoa is a rich source for protein, B vitamins, essential amino acids, iron, and fatty acids.

2 cups (500 ml.) water
1 cup (225 gm.) quinoa, rinsed
1 tsp. (4 gm.) basil or oregano
Pinch pepper

Bring the water to a boil and add the quinoa and spices. Reduce heat, cover, and simmer for 15-20 minutes. Fluff with a fork, let stand 8-10 minutes, then serve. Serves 4.

Tip: Use as a side dish or add to other recipes as a substitute for rice. Always rinse quinoa to remove the acrid taste.

QUINOA PILAF AND VEGETABLES

The Incan farmers in Peru were the first to harvest quinoa.
The popularity of quinoa is spreading and now many enjoy nourishing
recipes like this as a luncheon meal or a dinner side dish.

1 tbsp. (15 ml.) canola oil
1 small onion, chopped
2 carrots, chopped
2 cups (500 ml.) water
1 cup (225 gm.) quinoa, rinsed and drained
1 vegetable bouillon cube
1 tsp. (4 gm.) pumpkin pie spice or substitute ½ tsp. (2 gm.)
   each of cinnamon and cardamom
1 tbsp. (15 ml.) lemon juice
½ cup (115 gm.) raisins

In a medium-sized saucepan, heat the oil over medium heat. Add the onion and carrots and stir-fry for 2 minutes. Add the water, quinoa, and bouillon and stir and bring to a boil. Cover, reduce heat to low, and cook for 20 minutes. Stir in the pumpkin pie spice, lemon juice, and raisins. Cover and let stand 5 minutes before serving. Serves 4.

BULGUR WHEAT

Armenian folklore proclaims their traditional longevity was attributed
to their diet: whole wheat, matzoon (yogurt), and dried fruit.
Bulgur is rich in B vitamins and iron.

1½ cups (375 ml.) boiling water
½ tsp. (2 gm.) salt
1 cup (225 gm.) bulgur

Add the salt and bulgur to the boiling water, turn off heat, cover, and let stand for 30 minutes. Serves 2-3.

Note: Cooked bulgur can be substituted for rice as a side dish or as an ingredient in recipes calling for rice, such as stuffed peppers. It can be eaten as a cereal (just add sweetner and milk). Or it can be used in Taboule Salad.

TABOULE SALAD

If you use chilled cooked bulgur, the salad is prepared in just minutes.

2 cups (450 gm.) cooked bulgur
2 tbsp. (30 ml.) lemon juice
2 tbsp. (30 ml.) olive oil
1 tsp. (4 gm.) minced garlic
1 large tomato, finely chopped
½ cucumber, peeled and chopped
½ cup (115 gm.) fresh parsley, chopped
2 green onion stalks, chopped
1 tbsp. (15 gm.) dried mint
Lettuce

Add the lemon juice, olive oil, and garlic to the cooked bulgur; stir, cover, and chill in the refrigerator for at least 2 hours. Add the chopped vegetables and mint, toss well, and serve on beds of lettuce. Serves 4.

Hint: Available in most natural food stores and supermarkets are taboule salad mixes that speed up the process. However, when preparing bulgur, we recommend that you make double of the Bulgur Wheat recipe, prepare the taboule salad, and refrigerate the leftovers for other recipes.

TABOULE AND ARTICHOKE HEARTS SALAD

Simply delicious!

1 pkg. (5.25 oz. [149 gm.]) taboule wheat salad mix
1 tbsp. (15 ml.) olive oil*
1 large tomato, chopped into ½-inch (1.25-cm.) cubes
Juice of ½ lemon
1 jar (6 oz. [170 gm.]) marinated artichoke hearts, chopped

Prepare the taboule according to package directions. Toss in the olive oil, tomato, lemon juice, and artichoke hearts. Serve warm or chill for several hours before serving. Serves 4.

*If preferred, substitute the marinated artichoke heart liquid for the olive oil.

BULGUR PILAF

The Armenian upheaval of conquests by other cultures became a "culinary boon." This Turkish-Armenian dish is a good example.

2 tbsp. (30 ml.) olive oil
1 cup (225 gm.) mushrooms
1 onion, chopped
Pinch saffron
2 tsp. (8 gm.) dried basil
1 bay leaf
¼ tsp. (1 gm.) salt
⅛ tsp. (.5 gm.) pepper
1½ cups (340 gm.) raw bulgur wheat
2 cups (500 ml.) warm water
2 tsp. (10 ml.) blackstrap molasses

Heat the olive oil in a medium-sized saucepan and sauté the vegetables for 2 to 3 minutes. Stir in the saffron and cook for 1 minute. Add the remaining spices and sauté for 3 to 5 minutes. Add the bulgur and stir for 2 minutes (the bulgur will darken slightly). Add the water and molasses, bring to a boil, and stir once or twice. Cover the pan and reduce the heat to very low and steam for 20 minutes. Remove the bay leaf before serving. Serves 4.

Hint: Serve with fresh sliced tomatoes or a small salad. Vegans might want to sauté carrots and celery with the mushrooms and onions for a complete meal.

BULGUR AND LENTIL PILAF

A delicious blend with a double shot of B vitamins

1 cup (225 gm.) bulgur
1 cup (225 gm.) lentils
6 cups (1.5 l.) water
2 cloves garlic
½ tsp. (2 gm.) cumin
¼ tsp. (1 gm.) cayenne pepper
1 onion, finely chopped
1 tbsp. (15 ml.) olive oil
Salt and pepper to taste

Put all ingredients, except salt and pepper, in a large saucepan. Bring to a boil, cover, lower heat, and let simmer for 20 minutes. Turn off heat and let stand 10 minutes. Salt and pepper to taste. Serves 4.

LENTILS AND RICE (ITALIAN VERSION)

The Italians use lentils and rice for a cold salad.

½ cup (115 gm.) lentils
1 cup (250 ml.) water
½ tsp. (2 gm.) salt
1 cup (225 gm.) cooked rice
3 Roma (plum) tomatoes, chopped fine,
    or substitute 1 large tomato
¼ cup (60 gm.) bell pepper, chopped fine,
    or substitute 1 celery stalk
¼ cup (60 gm.) onion, chopped fine
4 or 5 green onions, sliced thin
½ cup (125 ml.) prepared Italian dressing
¼ cup (60 gm.) fresh parsley, chopped

Wash lentils and drain. In a heavy saucepan add lentils, water, and salt; bring to a boil, lower heat, cover, and simmer 15-20 minutes. Drain. Combine lentils with the remaining ingredients, except the parsley. Mix well and refrigerate 2 hours or more. Garnish with parsley before serving. Serves 3-4.

LENTILS AND RICE (EASTERN VERSION)

The garam masala spice (found in Indian food markets,
or the international section of supermarkets) makes this meal
so exotic that guests will think you were in the kitchen for hours.

1 cup (225 gm.) lentils
2½ tbsp. (35 gm.) ghee or butter
1 large onion, finely sliced
1 cup (225 gm.) long-grain rice
5 cups (1.25 l.) hot water
1 tsp. (4 gm.) salt
1½ tsp. (6 gm.) garam masala

Wash lentils and drain. Heat ghee in a large saucepan and sauté the onions until they are golden brown. Remove ¼ of the chopped onion and set aside for garnish.

Add lentils and rice to the sautéed onions and stir 2 to 3 minutes. Add hot water, salt, and garam masala. Bring to a boil and cover pan tightly. Reduce heat and simmer 25 minutes. Garnish with reserved onions. Serves 4-5.

Variations: With the onion, sauté one or more chopped vegetable(s): green pepper, celery, or carrots. For a stronger flavor, use vegetable broth instead of water.

FRIED RICE

Always prepare an extra amount of rice needed
to use in a recipe such as this, Fried Rice.

2 tbsp. (30 ml.) vegetable oil
1 green bell pepper, chopped
½ cup (115 gm.) fresh mushrooms, sliced
3 cups (680 gm.) cooked cold rice, white or brown
2 eggs, optional
1 to 2 tbsp. (15 to 30 ml.) soy sauce to taste

Heat the oil in a heavy, large skillet on medium-high heat. Sauté pepper and mushrooms for 2 to 3 minutes. Add the rice and stir constantly for 5 minutes. Make a well in the middle of the rice-vegetable mixture and add the eggs. Cook, stirring until scrambled, and mix into the rice-vegetable mixture. Sprinkle with soy sauce and stir. Serves 4.

Hint: Substitute with other vegetables or add as desired. Other vegetables that taste delicious in fried rice are green onions, broccoli, peas, or carrots. A great way to use leftover vegetables! For a juicier version of fried rice, add a cup of vegetable stock after sautéing the vegetables.

VEGETABLE RICE

Serve at dinnertime or reheat for lunch

3 tbsp. (45 ml.) canola oil
2 cups (450 gm.) long-grain rice
½ onion
2 garlic cloves, chopped
4 cups (1 l.) water
1 pkg. (10 oz. [284 gm.]) frozen mixed vegetables
1 tsp. (4 gm.) salt
½ tsp. (2 gm.) pepper

Heat the oil in a large, heavy saucepan. Add the rice, onion, and garlic and sauté until the rice is light brown. Add the water, mixed vegetables, and salt. Cover pan and bring to a boil. Reduce heat and simmer 20 to 25 minutes. Turn off heat and sprinkle with pepper. Serves 5-6.

VARIATIONS

- Add a vegetable bouillon with the water for extra flavor
- Reduce water by one cup and substitute with tomato sauce or tomato juice

RICE RECIPE VARIATIONS

Experiment with basmati or brown rice, long,
or short grain for a whole new flavor for each basic recipe.

RAISIN RICE

1 cup (225 gm.) rice
2 cups (500 ml.) vegetable stock
1 tbsp. (15 gm.) butter
½ cup (115 gm.) green raisins
½ tsp. (2 gm.) salt
¼ cup (60 gm.) toasted almonds, silvered

Combine all of the ingredients, except almonds, in a saucepan. Stir and bring to a boil. Cover and simmer 20 minutes. Add almonds and toss lightly. Serves 4.

CURRY AND CELERY RICE

1 cup (225 gm.) rice
½ tsp. (2 gm.) salt
2 cups (500 ml.) water or vegetable stock
½ tsp. (2 gm.) curry powder
1 stalk celery (leaves removed), finely chopped
¼ cup (60 gm.) toasted slivered almonds

Combine rice, salt, and water. Bring to a boil, cover, and simmer 20 minutes. Remove the cooked rice from heat and stir in curry powder and celery. Cover pan and let stand 5 minutes. Sprinkle almonds on top of servings. Serves 4.

Note: Basmati rice is the least tampered with pesticides because it is usually grown in more natural settings (the premier growing region is in the foothills of the Himalayas). Consequently, it is essential that basmati rice is rinsed thoroughly before cooking.

SAFFRON RICE

4 tsp. (20 ml.) vegetable oil
½ onion, finely chopped
1 cup (225 gm.) rice
2 cups (500 ml.) water
1 vegetable bouillon cube
Small pinch saffron
½ tsp. (2 gm.) salt

In a medium saucepan, on medium-high, heat the oil. Add the onion and sauté for 2 to 3 minutes. Add the remaining ingredients. Reduce heat, cover, and cook 20 minutes. Let stand, covered, 5 to 8 minutes. Serves 4.

PEANUTS AND RICE

2 tbsp. (30 ml.) peanut oil
2 cups (450 gm.) rice
3 cups (750 ml.) hot water
½ cup (115 gm.) peanuts
½ tsp. (2 gm.) garam masala

Heat oil in a heavy saucepan. Put rice in and stir until rice is golden, approximately 10 minutes. Add hot water and bring to a boil. Cover, reduce heat, and simmer 20 minutes. Add peanuts and garam masala, cover, and let stand 5 minutes. Serves 4.

RICE PILAF WITH PINE NUTS

2 tbsp. (30 gm.) butter
½ cup (115 gm.) pine nuts
1 cup (225 gm.) long-grain rice
1 tsp. (4 gm.) salt
1 stalk celery, chopped
2½ cups (625 ml.) vegetable broth

On medium heat, melt the butter in a heavy saucepan. Add the pine nuts and sauté until golden brown. Add the rice, salt, and celery and stir for 2 to 3 minutes; butter will be foamy and light amber. Add broth. Bring to a boil, cover, and simmer 25 minutes. Let stand, covered, 10 to 15 minutes. Serves 4.

(TVP®) TEXTURIZED VEGETABLE PROTEIN

Available in natural food stores and through mail order,* TVP® is a derivative of soybeans and a good source of protein, fiber, potassium, and essential amino acids. Unlike meat, TVP® has no cholesterol. TVP® is **not** *a source for B12, unless stated vitamin B12-fortified.*

CHUNK-SIZED TVP® (CONVENTIONAL METHOD)

1 cup (250 ml.) water or vegetable stock
1 tbsp. (15 gm.) ketchup or vinegar
1 cup (225 gm.) chunky TVP®

In a saucepan, bring the water to a boil, add the ketchup, and stir. Add TVP®, stir, cover, and let soak 5 minutes.

CHUNK-SIZED TVP® (MICROWAVE METHOD)

1 cup (250 ml.) water or vegetable stock
1 tbsp. (15 gm.) ketchup or vinegar
1 cup (225 gm.) chunky TVP®

In a microwave-safe bowl, mix the water, ketchup, and TVP®. Cover tightly with plastic wrap and cook on hight power for 5 to 6 minutes. Check after 2 minutes, and add a small amount of liquid if needed.

SMALL GRANULES TVP®

⅞ cup (200 ml.) boiling water
1 cup (225 gm.) TVP®

In a bowl, pour the boiling water over the TVP®. Stir and let stand 8 to 10 minutes.

*To order TVP® through the mail, write to The Mail Order Catalog, P.O. Box 180-TC, Summertown, TN 38483.

CHAPTER 4
Breakfast

Nutritionists and mothers all agree that this is the most important meal of the day. Yet, with most busy life-styles, it is the meal most often neglected. Individuals who protest, "I don't have an appetite for breakfast," usually mean they are too much in a hurry or are bored from years of the same cold cereal offerings. The recipes presented in this chapter will convert most hard-to-please breakfast dodgers.

BANANA FRENCH TOAST

High in protein, potassium, and A and B vitamins.
A great way to save a dying banana!

3 eggs
½ cup (125 ml.) low-fat milk
½ tsp. (2 gm.) nutmeg
1 ripe banana (more brown than yellow peel)
¼ tsp. (1 gm.) cinnamon
1 loaf of French bread sliced into ½-inch (1.25-cm.) slices

Mix all of the above ingredients (except the French bread) in a blender for 30 seconds. Pour the mixture into a pie pan.

Preheat the griddle on medium-high. *To test:* A sprinkle of water will sizzle on the griddle when the griddle has reached the right temperature. Use a light amount of canola oil to prevent sticking if you're not using a nonstick griddle.

Dip the French bread slices in the mixture and evenly coat both sides. Place the dipped bread on the griddle. Cook on both sides for approximately 45 seconds, or until golden brown. Sprinkle a light amount of confectionary sugar, garnish with your favorite fruit, and serve. Serves 4 to 6.

Hint: Leftover Banana French Toast can be wrapped in a paper towel, placed in a covered container, and later toasted. Make extra amounts for a quick breakfast or snack. To add variety, just change the topping. For example, spread on peanut butter or a mixture of nuts and syrup.

COCONUT PANCAKES

Too delicious to ever make regular pancakes again

1 egg
1½ cups (375 ml.) regular coconut milk
1 tbsp. (15 ml.) canola oil
1 tbsp. (15 gm.) sugar
1 cup (225 gm.) flour
1 tsp. (4 gm.) baking soda
½ tsp. (2 gm.) salt
½ tsp. (2 ml.) coconut flavoring for added flavor (optional)

Put all ingredients into a blender and mix until smooth. Heat a lightly oiled griddle on medium-high heat. Pour a small amount of batter for each pancake on the griddle. Cook until pancakes are lightly brown. Flip pancakes over and brown on reverse side. Serves 2 to 3.

Note: Do not use light coconut milk.

BREAKFAST FRUIT STRATA

*Prepare in the evening and microwave it in 8 minutes
the next morning for a delicious breakfast treat.*

**8 large slices French, sourdough, or a light wheat bread, crusts
   trimmed**
1 cup (225 gm.) chunky style applesauce*
¼ cup (60 gm.) walnuts
4 eggs
1½ cups (375 ml.) milk
1½ tsp. (6 gm.) cinnamon

Tear 4 slices of bread into large pieces and place in the bottom of a lightly buttered 8-by-8-inch glass baking dish. Spread the applesauce evenly over the bread. Sprinkle walnuts over the applesauce.

Whisk together the eggs and milk. Pour over the bread/fruit mixture. Tear the remaining slices of bread into large pieces and place them on top. Cover with plastic wrap and refrigerate overnight. In the morning, remove the plastic wrap and cover with a paper towel. Microwave on high power for 8 minutes. Serves 4 to 5.

*Substitute with favorite fruit pie filling.

Hint: Serve with Baked Bananas.

BAKED BANANAS

High in potassium and satisfies a sweet tooth

2 tbsp. (30 gm.) butter
3 tbsp. (45 ml.) maple syrup
4 bananas
½ tsp. (2 gm.) cinnamon
Juice of ½ lemon

In a medium-size microwave-safe baking dish, microwave the butter on high power for 30 seconds. Stir in the maple syrup. Place the bananas in the dish and baste with the butter-maple syrup mixture. Sprinkle the cinnamon on the bananas. Microwave on high for 1 minute. Turn the bananas and cook for another minute. Squeeze the lemon juice over the bananas. Serves 4.

COUSCOUS FOR A HONEY BREAKFAST

This breakfast, prepared in 6 to 7 minutes, provides one-third of the daily requirements for protein and vitamins A and B.

1 cup (250 ml.) water
1 thin slice of butter
1 cup (225 gm.) couscous
1 tsp. (5 ml.) honey
1 cup (250 ml.) milk

Add the butter to the water in a small saucepan; bring to a boil and add the couscous. Stir 3 times. Turn the heat off, cover the saucepan, and let stand for 5 minutes. Add honey and let stand for 1 minute. Stir once or twice before pouring into 4 cereal bowls. Pour desired amount of milk in each bowl. Buttermilk or low-fat milk can be used if calorie intake is a concern. Serves 4.

Hint: Couscous can be prepared in the microwave oven—follow directions on the package. Also, couscous can be reheated in the microwave oven.

CUSH-CUSH

Originally an American Indian dish popularized by Louisianians

1 cup (225 gm.) yellow cornmeal
¼ cup (60 gm.) baking mix, such as Bisquick
1 tbsp. (15 gm.) sugar
⅔ cup (160 ml.) water
½ cup (30 ml.) canola oil
¼ cup (60 ml.) milk
1 tbsp. (15 gm.) butter

Combine the cornmeal, baking mix, and sugar and slowly stir in the water. In a nonstick, medium-sized saucepan, on medium-low heat, add the oil, then the cornmeal mixture; cover and cook 5 minutes. Uncover, reduce heat to very low, and cook 5-6 minutes, stirring occasionally. Remove from heat and add the milk and butter. Cover and let stand 1 or 2 minutes. Serve with either maple syrup, molasses, or milk. Serves 2.

MIDDLE EASTERN OMELET

Exotic flavors give new meaning to an omelet.

5 eggs
1 tsp. (4 gm.) curry powder
Dash milk (optional)
1 tbsp. (15 ml.) olive oil
¼ cup (60 gm.) onions
¼ cup (60 gm.) mushrooms
2 falafel balls,* cooked as directed on pkg. and crumbled
½ cup (115 gm.) of grated mozzarella cheese, optional

In a small bowl, beat the eggs lightly with the curry and milk. Heat the oil in an omelet pan; pour in the egg mixture. Add the onions, mushrooms, crumbled falafel, and cheese. Lift the edges of the egg and let the uncooked egg spill over until the top is almost set. Fold the omelet and transfer to two plates. Serves 2.

*Prepare a 10-oz. (284 gm.) pkg., which makes 48 1-inch (2.5-cm.) balls, and store the remaining falafel balls in the refrigerator to use later in pocket-bread sandwiches.

CONGLOMERATE OMELET

Warning! Prepare only when you have an empty stomach.

6 eggs
2 tbsp. (30 ml.) milk
2 tbsp. (30 gm.) butter
1 small tomato, chopped
¼ onion, chopped
½ red or green bell pepper, chopped
4 mushrooms, sliced
¼ cup (60 gm.) grated cheddar cheese
¼ cup (60 gm.) salsa
Salt and pepper to taste

In a small bowl, lightly beat the eggs and milk. Melt the butter in a heavy, medium-size skillet over medium heat. Pour in the egg mixture. Spoon the remaining ingredients in the center of the egg mixture. Lift the edges of the egg and let the uncooked egg flow under until the top is almost set. Lift one-half of the omelet and fold over. Cut the folded omelet in half with the edge of the spatula. Transfer each omelet half to a plate. Serves 2.

VEGETABLE FRITTATA

Frittatas are just like an omelet but are not folded
Serve the frittata as the complete meal for breakfast, or
as the base for an antipasto salad and serve for lunch or dinner.

3 tbsp. (45 ml.) olive oil
1 zucchini, chopped
1 carrot, chopped
1 onion, chopped
6 eggs
½ tsp. (2 gm.) dried basil
Salt and pepper to taste

Heat the oil on medium heat in a 10-inch skillet. Add the zucchini, carrot, and onion; sauté for approximately 5 minutes, stirring often.

While the vegetables are sautéing, beat the eggs slightly and add the basil, salt, and pepper. Spread the vegetables evenly on bottom of the pan and pour the eggs over them. Reduce the heat to very low and cover the skillet. Cook for 15-20 minutes. While cooking, check to see if the frittata is puffing up in a large bubble. If so, pierce the bubble with a sharp knife once or twice.

If the eggs are firm on top, loosen the frittata slowly by sliding a spatula underneath it. Place a plate upside down over the top of the skillet. Overturn the skillet quickly, so that the frittata falls out onto the plate. Slide the frittata back into the skillet with the top side down to brown for a few minutes. Turn the frittata back onto the plate and serve immediately. Serves 3-4.

Variations: Add or substitute vegetables such as mushrooms, eggplant, summer squash, bell pepper, or broccoli. Try serving with your favorite salsa or grated cheese.

TEX-MEX POTATOES AND TOFU

A hearty breakfast with traditional Tex-Mex flavor

1 pkg. (2 lbs. [900 gm.]) frozen hashed brown potatoes
⅓ cup (80 ml.) canola oil
Salt and pepper to taste
1 pkg. (14-16 oz. [397 to 450 gm.]) tofu, cut in ¼-inch
    (.65-cm.) cubes
½ onion (red or yellow), chopped fine
½ green bell pepper, chopped fine
1 can (15 oz. [425 gm.]) black beans,* drained
1 cup (225 gm.) salsa
1 cup (225 gm.) cheddar cheese, shredded

In a large, heavy skillet, heat the oil. Add the potatoes and cook according to directions. Season with the salt and pepper. Add the tofu, onion, and pepper and stir-fry for 3 minutes. Reduce the heat, add the beans, and stir-fry for 2 minutes. Top each serving with salsa and cheese. Serves 6.

*To stoke the "get up and go" fire, substitute S&W® HOT Chili Beans and Chipotle Peppers or another similar brand for the black beans.

BANANA BREAKFAST PUDDING

A good way to start the day—dessert for breakfast.
Drink a glass of juice and eat a bran muffin for a complete meal.

3 eggs
1 cup (250 ml.) sweetened condensed milk*
1 tsp. (5 ml.) vanilla
3 bananas
Nutmeg

Put the eggs, milk, vanilla, and bananas in the blender. Process on blend until well blended. Pour the mixture into a small, nonstick saucepan, cover, and cook on very low heat for about 20 minutes; the sauce will thicken. Place in individual serving bowls and lightly sprinkle with nutmeg. Serves 4.

*If preferred, substitute regular coconut milk and add ½ cup (115 gm.) sugar.

Hint 1: While the pudding is steaming, take a shower.

Hint 2: To sweeten a serving of cooked bulgur wheat, stir in a few tablespoons of Banana Breakfast Pudding and heat in the microwave for 2 minutes. Add milk if desired.

REFRIGERATED BRAN MUFFINS

The batter can be stored in the refrigerator for up to six weeks.

**1 box (15 oz. [425 gm.]) raisin bran cereal
5 cups (1.134 kg.) unbleached white flour
1 cup (225 gm.) sugar
5 tsp. (20 gm.) baking soda
2 tsp. (8 gm.) salt
4 eggs
½ cup (125 ml.) canola oil
1 cup (250 ml.) molasses
1 qt. (1 l.) buttermilk**

Preheat the oven to 350 degrees (177 degrees Celsius).

In an extra-large bowl, mix the cereal, flour, sugar, baking soda, and salt together. In a separate bowl, hand-beat or whisk the eggs; add the oil, molasses, and buttermilk; and beat until mixed. Pour the liquids into the dry ingredients. Mix until well blended. Fill greased or pretreated muffin tins half-full with batter. Bake for 20 minutes in the preheated oven. Makes 5½-6 dozen large bran muffins.

Note: You can store the batter in the refrigerator for up to six weeks or bake all of the batter at once and freeze the fresh-baked muffins.

OATMEAL MUFFINS

Easy to prepare and bakes in only 15 minutes

1¼ cups (285 gm.) whole wheat flour
½ tsp. (2 gm.) salt
3 tsp. (12 gm.) baking powder
½ tsp. (2 gm.) cinnamon
1 cup (225 gm.) rolling oats
1 egg, slightly beaten
¼ cup (60 ml.) molasses
3 tbsp. (45 ml.) canola oil
½ cup (115 gm.) raisins (optional)

Preheat the oven to 450 degrees (232 degrees Celsius).

Place the flour, salt, and baking powder in a large bowl. Add the remaining ingredients; stir just enough to blend. Fill greased or pretreated muffin tins two-thirds full. Bake for 15 minutes in the preheated oven. Makes 12.

TOFU WAFFLES

Crunchy waffles that freeze well and can be toasted for quick-power starts

1¼ cups (300 ml.) milk
1 pkg. (14-16 oz. [400-450 gm.]) tofu
2 tbsp. (30 ml.) honey
½ tsp. (2 gm.) salt
1 tsp. (4 gm.) baking powder
½ tsp. (2 gm.) cinnamon
1 cup (225 gm.) whole wheat flour

Preheat the waffle iron while preparing the waffle mix. Put all of the ingredients in the blender and mix until smooth. Bake in the waffle iron according to manufacturer's directions. Makes 4 large waffles.

Hint: Double the recipe to have extra to freeze.

DOSAS (CREPES FROM INDIA)

They can be served plain or filled with chutney.

1 cup (225 gm.) urhad dal (lentils)
¼ cup (60 gm.) rice
2½ cups (625 ml.) water
½ tsp. (2 gm.) baking soda
1 tsp. (4 gm.) chili powder
½ tsp. (2 gm.) salt
Vegetable oil for frying

Wash and drain the dal and rice. Put them in a large bowl, stir in the water, and let soak overnight. The next morning place the dal-rice mixture in an electric blender or food processor and mix until smooth. Add the baking soda, chili powder, and salt and stir until mixed.

Heat a small amount of oil in a heavy, medium-sized skillet over medium-high heat. After the pan is hot, pour in enough batter to cover the bottom of the skillet. Fry until golden brown and turn once; brown on the other side. Remove from the pan and roll like a crepe. Continue to fry and roll until all of the batter is used. Serve plain or fill with a small layer of applesauce or chutney. Serves 10-12.

TWO-MINUTE BREAKFASTS

BRAN MUFFIN

Homemade or store-bought, a bran muffin satisfies the appetite.

1 bran muffin
1 tbsp. (15 gm.) cream cheese or 1 tsp. (4 gm.) butter

Wrap the muffin in a paper towel and warm up in the microwave for 20-25 seconds. Cut the muffin in half and spread with either cream cheese or butter. If necessary because of time constraint, rewrap the bran muffin in the paper towel, grab a banana, and eat a healthy breakfast as you drive to your destination.

Hint: Store bran muffins or bagels in the freezer for good, fast food.

GRANOLA AND YOGURT

This is fast food without waiting in a slow moving drive-through!

1 cup (225 gm.) plain yogurt
¼ cup (60 gm.) granola
½ cup (115 gm.) fresh fruit, optional

Stir the yogurt, granola, and fruit together in a small bowl. Serves 1.

Tip: Yogurt is a healthy food that fights colds, soothes a sensitive stomach (even for those with a lactose intolerance), is chock full of calcium to help prevent osteoporosis, curbs vaginal yeast infections, and is now linked to lowering the risk of breast cancer in women.

YOGURT DRINK

Whip up in seconds

½ cup (115 gm.) plain yogurt
½ cup (125 ml.) orange juice
2 tbsp. (30 gm.) wheat germ
2 ice cubes

Whip all of the ingredients in a blender until foamy. Pour and drink. Serves 1.

CASHEW NUT MILK

A substitute for cow's milk or a "fast lane" nutritious drink.

⅔ cup (90 gm.) cashew nuts
1 cup (250 ml.) warm water
1 tbsp. (15 ml.) molasses
1 tsp. (4 gm.) lecithin granules (optional)

In a blender, add the cashews and grind until finely chopped. Add the water, molasses, and lecithin. Blend on high speed, or "liquify" setting, until creamy. Strain if using for cooking purposes. Refrigerate until ready to seve. Makes about 1½ cups (375 ml.).

Hint: You can add ½ cup (115 gm.) of your favorite berries for a change of flavor.

RICHARD'S NUTTY CHOCOLATE DRINK

High protein for a morning jump start or afternoon revitalizer

Nutty Chocolate Protein Mix

⅓ cup (90 gm.) ground almonds
1 tbsp. (15 gm.) ground flaxseed
2 tbsp. (30 gm.) ground sunflower seeds
¼ cup (60 gm.) whey
2 tbsp. (30 ml.) fructose
1 tbsp. (15 gm.) cocoa powder
¼ cup (60 ml.) carob powder
1 tsp. (4 gm.) alm powder

The ingredients can be purchased at most natural food stores. Mix the ingredients in a glass jar and tighten. Store in the refrigerator. This is enough protein mix for a week's supply.

For One Serving:

Add 3 tbsp. of the nutty chocolate protein mix to 1½ cups (125 ml.) milk, or substitute a soy beverage or rice milk for the milk. Process in the blender on blend for 1 minute. For a smooth version, pour contents through a strainer into a glass and serve.

Notes from Travis: I dedicate this drink to my roommate and good friend. Although he will never become a dedicated vegetarian, he has become health conscious and enjoys this drink immensely. A liquid that gives you more than half of your daily protein requirement, this recipe is also loaded with vitamins A and B series.

BASIC PROTEIN DRINK

An instant protein drink that contains a heaping amount of daily nutrient requirements.

Protein Drink Mix

½ cup (115 gm.) ground almonds
½ cup (115 gm.) ground cashews
2 tbsp. (30 gm.) ground flaxseeds
2 tbsp. (30 gm.) ground raw sunflower seeds
1 tbsp. (15 gm.) lecithin granules
1 tbsp. (15 gm.) slippery elm powder
1 tbsp. (15 gm.) whey

Grind all of the nuts and seeds, mix all of the ingredients, pour into a container with an airtight lid, and store in the refrigerator.

For One Serving of Basic Protein Drink:

1½ cups (375 ml.) organic soy beverage, or milk
1 tbsp. (15 ml.) honey or molasses
½ tsp. (2 ml.) vanilla
½ of a banana, or ½ cup (115 gm.) fruit*
3 tbsp. (45 gm.) Protein Drink Mix

Pour the soy beverage or milk, honey or molasses, vanilla, and fruit into a blender; add the Protein Drink Mix and process on blend for 1 minute. Process again on whip or high speed for 30 seconds. Pour into a tall glass.

*Fresh or frozen fruit (thawed) such as strawberries, blueberries, or blackberries

Note: This recipe can be modified for individual needs. Below is information about the different nuts and seeds that can be substituted in the basic recipe.

Nuts (almonds, brazil, cashews, pecans, walnuts, and peanuts): A high source of protein, unsaturated fat, B-complex vitamins, iron, potassium, magnesium, manganese, phosphorous, and copper.

Seeds (flaxseeds; sunflower, pumpkin, and sesame seeds; and pine nuts): A good source for protein, B-complex vitamins, vitamins A, D, and E, and minerals.

Extra rich sources of nutrients: Almonds—calcium and magnesium; pumpkin seeds—magnesium and zinc; peanuts—biotin and potassium; sesame seeds—calcium and selenium.

Note from Travis: The Basic Protein Drink is for vegetarians who always wanted to gain weight in the form of muscle. This drink offers more than 1,000 calories with minimal saturated fat. You can expect to get 75 percent of your needed protein in one glass and it's all natural. I've spent a lot of time, money, and research in developing a purely natural and healthy protein drink that is not laden with sugars. The soy beverage adds linoleic, an unsaturated fatty acid, essential for healthy blood, arteries (it breaks down and transports cholesterol), nerves, and youthful skin (prevents dryness).

MONKEY MASH

Bananas to expensive, highly sugared, prepared breakfast drinks.
Prepare in 2 minutes with ingredients you usually have on hand.

1 banana
1 egg (optional)
1 tbsp. (15 gm.) wheat germ
¼ cup (60 gm.) walnuts
1 cup (250 ml.) whole or low-fat milk
1 tsp. (5 ml.) vanilla

Put all of the ingredients in a blender. Cover and process on whip or high speed for 1 minute.

Hint: ½ cup (115 gm.) of fresh fruit in season can be added to vary the flavor. Molasses can also be added to increase your iron intake.

SASSY MOLASSES DRINK

Molasses is a natural sweetner high in iron
with traces of calcium and B1.

1 tbsp. (15 ml.) molasses
1 cup (250 ml.) whole or low-fat milk

Stir the molasses and milk together in a tall glass until blended. Serve cold. Sassy Molasses can be "Soothing Molasses" if you heat your milk and drink just before retiring for sleep. Serves 1.

VEGGIE-FRUIT LIQUID BOOST

Cool and refreshing for a quick energy boost

¼ cucumber, peeled and sliced
½ carrot, chopped
1 stalk celery with a few leaves, chopped
1 cup (250 ml.) unsweetened tropical juice* (choose fresh,
**   prepared frozen, or canned)**
Dash of Tabasco® sauce or a pinch of cayenne pepper

Process in juicer or blender until the vegetables are liquified. Pour into a glass with a few ice cubes. Serves 1. Increase ingredients proportionately to serve more.

*Use pineapple, mango, guava or a mixture of tropical juices.

Tip: As with all citrus beverages, drink immediately before oxygen breaks down the nutrients.

PINE NUT DRINK

A sweet treat to refresh and fuel the body

2 tbsp. (30 gm.) pine nuts, crushed
2 tsp. (10 gm.) whey
½ tsp. (2 gm.) soy granules
½ tsp. (2 gm.) flaxseed
½ tsp. (2 ml.) molasses
1 cup (250 ml.) milk*

Put all of the ingredients into a blender. Cover and process on whip or high speed for 1 minute. Pour into a tall glass. Serves 1.

*If desired, substitute with rice or soy beverage

OTHER FAST BREAKFAST IDEAS

Add fruit and juice to the selections for a nutritional meal.

- Whole grain or bran cold cereal with milk
- Instant oatmeal (cooks in the microwave oven in two minutes); add raisins, bananas, or walnuts for more variety and nutrition
- Peanut butter spread on whole wheat toast
- Leftover French toast warmed in the toaster
- A leftover staple like bulgur, couscous, kashi, or rice. Reheat in the microwave, add milk, fruit juice, dried fruit, nuts, or sweetner.

CHAPTER 5
Lunch

Lunch can be the most sociable meal of the day. It is the time spent in lunchrooms, cafeterias, and outdoor patios at work or school. Most businesses now have microwave ovens in the cafeterias to accommodate for meals brought to work. Whether it is a recipe from this chapter, a soup, or a leftover dinner "brown bagged," co-workers or school friends will consider converting to a vegetarian diet after watching you, day after day, enjoy so many tantalizing lunches.

DILLED MACARONI SALAD

A dilly way to enjoy lunch

1 pkg. (8 oz. [225 gm.]) elbow macaroni
2 stalks green onions, chopped
4 stalks celery, chopped
1 cucumber, peeled and sliced
½ cup (125 ml.) evaporated skimmed milk
3 tbsp. (45 ml.) white vinegar
1 tsp. (4 gm.) mustard
2 tsp. (8 gm.) sugar
1 tsp. (4 gm.) dried dillweed
½ tsp. (2 gm.) salt
¼ tsp. (1 gm.) pepper

Prepare the macaroni according to package directions. Drain, rinse in cold water, and drain in colander. Place drained macaroni, onions, celery, and cucumber in a large bowl and set aside.

Combine all of the other ingredients in a jar. Cover tightly and shake briskly. Pour the dressing over the macaroni and vegetables and toss gently. Cover and chill in the refrigerator for at least two hours. Serves 4-5.

ITALIAN SALAD

Pasta and Italian herbs make this a favorite lunch salad.

1 pkg. (8 oz. [225 gm.]) spinach rotini pasta, cooked and
    drained
1 can (15 oz. [425 gm.]) stewed Italian tomatoes, undrained
1 jar (6 oz. [170 gm.]) marinated artichoke hearts, undrained
½ cup (115 gm.) pitted black olives, sliced
½ red onion, finely chopped
½ tsp. (2 gm.) dried basil
½ tsp. (2 gm.) dried oregano
2 tbsp. (30 gm.) grated Parmesan cheese
2 tbsp. (30 ml.) wine vinegar
½ tsp. (2 gm.) salt
¼ tsp. (1 gm.) red pepper flakes (optional)

Place all ingredients in a bowl. Toss to thoroughly mix. Refrigerate for several hours or overnight before serving. Serves 6.

BAKED TOMATOES

*Fight the blahs with a colorful lunch prepared
the evening before and reheated in the microwave.*

½ cup (115 gm.) plain yogurt
1½ tsp. (6 mg.) flour
½ tsp. (2 mg.) basil
½ tsp. (2 mg.) salt
¼ tsp. (1 mg.) pepper
½ cup (115 gm.) cooked staple (brown rice, kasha, couscous)
2 large red tomatoes
1 tbsp. (15 ml.) canola oil
¼ cup (60 gm.) Romano or Parmesan cheese, grated

Preheat the oven to 400 degrees (204 degrees Celsius).

Combine the yogurt, flour, basil, salt, pepper, and staple; mix well and set aside.

Cut each tomato in half crosswise and remove the seeds. Grease an 8-inch (20-cm.) baking dish with the oil and insert the four tomato shells, cut sides up. Spoon in equal amounts of the yogurt-staple mixture in each tomato half. Sprinkle each tomato with cheese. Bake for 30 minutes in the preheated oven. Serves 4.

CREAMY ASPARAGUS

Watch your co-workers drool as you reheat another delicious meal at lunchtime in the cafeteria microwave.

3 cups (675 gm.) asparagus, cut into large pieces
2 tbsp. (30 gm.) butter
2 tbsp. (30 gm.) flour
½ cup (125 ml.) whole milk
½ cup (125 ml.) asparagus liquid
3 hard-boiled eggs, sliced thin
¼ tsp. (1 gm.) nutmeg

In a medium saucepan, cover the asparagus with water and bring to a boil. Reduce heat and simmer 8 minutes. Remove asparagus and set aside. Reserve ½ cup (125 ml.) of the asparagus liquid. In the same saucepan, melt the butter. Blend in the flour while stirring constantly. Add the milk and asparagus liquid. Heat just to a boil. Add the asparagus and the eggs. Season with the nutmeg. Serve over cooked noodles. Creamy Asparagus can also be served over toast or a bagel. Serves 2.

GARBANZO PATTIES

Prepare the patties in the evening and bring to work the next day.
Top with a sliced tomato or salsa, or use as a base for Creamy Asparagus
(see recipe). These patties are to be eaten without a bun.

1 cup (250 ml.) water
½ cup (125 ml.) milk
1½ cups (340 gm.) instant mashed potato flakes
1 tbsp. (15 gm.) margarine
1 can (15-16 oz. [425-450 gm.]) garbanzos, drained and mashed
1 tsp. (4 gm.) coriander
2 tsp. A.1.® Steak Sauce
2 tbsp. (30 ml.) canola oil

In a medium-sized saucepan, bring the water and milk to a boil. Turn the heat off and stir in the potato flakes and margarine. Stir until smooth. Or follow the package directions on the potatoes and adjust the water and milk for the total liquid amount.

Stir in the garbanzos, coriander, and A.1.® Steak Sauce until well blended.

Heat the oil on medium-high heat in a large, nonstick skillet. Form patties in the palm of your hand and place in the skillet. Brown on both sides, approximately 5 minutes on each side. Remove the patties and place on a paper towel to drain. Makes 6 patties.

CUCUMBER SANDWICH

A cool sandwich when the heat is high

3 tbsp. (45 ml.) mayonnaise
Dash cayenne pepper
2 slices dark bread
½ cucumber,* peeled and cut into ¼-inch (.65-cm.) thick slices
Dash salt
¼ cup (60 gm.) alfalfa sprouts

Mix the mayonnaise with the cayenne pepper; spread on one side of both slices of bread. Place the cucumber slices on the top of one slice of bread. Salt to taste. Top with alfalfa sprouts. Cover with the second slice of bread. Cover in plastic wrap or place in a sandwich container for lunch.

*Use the remaining cucumber for a salad or another dish.

Variation: Substitute tomato for cucumber.

VEGETARIAN HERO

The combination of a basil spread with artichoke hearts, provolone cheese, tomatoes, red onions, and fresh spinach will make the chef a hero.

1 cup (225 gm.) fresh basil leaves, stems removed
⅓ cup (80 ml.) virgin olive oil
¼ cup (60 gm.) walnuts
2 tbsp. (30 ml.) grated Parmesan cheese
1 tbsp. (15 ml.) white-wine vinegar
2 tsp. (10 ml.) Dijon mustard
1 clove garlic, quartered
1 loaf French bread, unsliced
1 can (14 oz. [400 gm.]) artichoke hearts, drained and sliced
4 oz. (115 gm.) sliced provolone cheese
1 large tomato, thinly sliced
1 medium red onion, thinly sliced
2 cups (450 gm.) fresh spinach leaves, torn

In a blender or food processor combine the basil, oil, walnuts, Parmesan cheese, vinegar, mustard, and garlic. Cover and blend until just smooth. Set aside.

Cut the French bread loaf in half lengthwise. Spread the basil mixture over each French bread half. On the bottom half, layer the artichoke hearts, provolone cheese, tomato, red onions, and spinach. Cover with the top bread half. Cut the sandwich loaf crosswise into 6-8 sections. Serves 6-8.

Hint: If crunched for time, use a prepared basil pesto sauce on this sandwich.

SUN-KISSED TOMATO SANDWICHES

Easy to prepare and easy to transport for away-from-home lunches

INDIVIDUAL SANDWICH

1 French roll (plain, sourdough, or whole wheat)
2 tbsp. (30 ml.) olive oil
4-5 sun-dried tomatoes, cooked (see below)
1 slice provolone cheese
1 lettuce leaf

Slice the French roll in half. Spoon on one tbsp. of olive oil over each cut half. On the bottom half place the cooked sun-dried tomatoes, a slice of cheese, and a lettuce leaf. Top with the second half of the French roll.

COOKED SUN-DRIED TOMATOES
STORED IN OLIVE OIL

1 pkg. (3 oz. [85 gm.]) sun-dried tomatoes
¼ cup (60 ml.) water
Virgin olive oil
Garlic slice
Herbs

Empty the package of sun-dried tomatoes into a small microwave container. Add ¼ cup (60 ml.) water. Cover and cook in the microwave oven on high power for 60 seconds. Drain the water. Place the cooked tomatoes in a small jar and pour enough olive oil into the jar to cover the tomatoes. Add a garlic slice and/or your choice of herb or herbs. Shake to evenly distribute the olive oil over the tomatoes. Refrigerate for 2-3 days.

Note: Sun-dried tomatoes that have marinated in olive oil can be drained, chopped, and used in salads, soups, pasta sauces, and for pizza toppings. The olive oil used to marinate the sun-dried tomatoes can also be used for salad dressings and pasta sauces. Supermarkets and food specialty stores have many choices of olive oil with herbs and spices already added to use to marinate the sun-dried tomatoes if you wish to look.

BAKED BEAN SANDWICH

*A Depression-era sandwich when meat was scarce,
but just as healthy then as it is today*

1 cup (225 gm.) baked beans from Baked Beans recipe*
¼ cup (60 gm.) walnuts, chopped
1 stalk celery, chopped
¼ onion, chopped
½ tsp. (2 gm.) salt
¼ cup (60 gm.) ketchup
2 tbsp. (30 gm.) pickle relish
8 thick slices of whole wheat bread

Mix all of the ingredients, except the bread. Spread the bean mixture evenly on 4 of the bread slices. Top each sandwich with a slice of bread. Serves 4.
*Substitute, if desired, prepared, canned vegetarian baked beans

SAUERKRAUT SANDWICH

This sandwich will make new vegetarians forget all about Reuben.

2 slices pumpernickel bread or dark rye bread
Mustard and/or mayonnaise
2 slices Swiss cheese
2 slices tomato
⅓ cup (90 gm.) sauerkraut, drained
1 pat butter

On one side of each slice of bread spread mustard and/or mayonnaise. Top one bread slice (spread side up) with cheese, tomato, and sauerkraut. Cover with the second slice of bread. Melt the butter in a small nonstick frying pan on medium-high heat. Place the sandwich in the frying pan and cook on one side until lightly browned. Flip the sandwich and fry on the second side until lightly browned and the cheese has melted. Serves 1.

Hint: If desired, add a prepared meatless patty (*see* the Veggie Burger).

PITA BREAD LUNCHES

There are many variations of fillings and toppings.

Fillings (recipes follow):

- Spinach-Water Chestnut Spread
- Spinach-Cream Cheese Spread
- Hummus
- Black Bean and Corn Mexican Filling
- Black Bean Filling
- Egg Salad Filling
- Taboule Salad (see recipe)
- Falafel Balls (prepare as directed on package)

Toppings

- Tomatoes
- Cucumbers
- Avocado
- Onions
- Lettuce
- Spinach
- Olives
- Sprouts
- Feta cheese
- Cheese, cubed or grated
- Marinated artichoke hearts

Sauces

- Tahini Sauce (see recipe), or a prepared version is available in Middle Eastern markets and natural food stores
- Vegetable Dip (see recipe)
- Cucumber Raita (see recipe)

Note: Pita-bread fillings, toppings and sauces should not be placed in the pita bread pocket until ready to eat. This keeps the pita bread from becoming too soggy to eat.

SPINACH-WATER CHESTNUT SPREAD

A lunch or snack treat with Popeye's seal of approval

1 pkg. (10 oz. [285 gm.]) frozen chopped spinach, defrosted
1 cup (225 gm.) mayonnaise or Miracle Whip®
1 cup (225 gm.) sour cream
1 can (8 oz. [225 gm.]) water chestnuts, sliced
1 pkg. dry vegetable soup or salad dressing mix

Mix all of the ingedients and refrigerate for several hours. Spread on slices of bread or on crackers, or use as a topping for pita-bread slices.

SPINACH-CREAM CHEESE FILLING

Interesting combination of food for health and flavor

1 pkg. (8 oz. [225 gm.]) cream cheese, softened
1 pkg. (10 oz. [285 gm.]) chopped frozen spinach, thawed
1 tbsp. (15 gm.) dried basil
2 cloves garlic, minced
¼ tsp. (1 gm.) salt
5 slices oil-marinated sun-dried tomatoes, drained and chopped
  into small pieces

In a blender or food processor process the cream cheese, spinach, basil, garlic, and salt until smooth. Add the tomatoes and stir by hand. Turn into a serving dish, cover, and chill for approximately one hour. Spread in a pita bread pocket or on whole wheat bread slices. Serves 4-6.

HUMMUS FILLING

The blender makes hummus in just a few whirls.

**1 can (15 oz. [425 gm.]) garbanzo beans, drain and reserve ¼
cup (60 ml.) liquid
2 tbsp. (30 ml.) lime or lemon juice
1 clove garlic, minced
2 tbsp. (30 ml.) olive oil
½ tsp. (2 gm.) salt**

In a food processor or blender, blend the garbanzo beans and reserved liquid for 1 minute. Add the lime juice, garlic, olive oil, and salt and blend until smooth. Cut the pita pocket in half. Spread the hummus inside and spoon in your choice of vegetables. Hummus can also be served as a dip used with wedges of fresh or toasted pita bread. Just transfer the prepared hummus to a bowl and sprinkle with paprika. Serves 6.

Note: For a spicy hummus flavor, add ¼ chopped red onion, 1 tbsp. (15 gm.) tahini, 1 tsp. (4 gm.) cumin, and a dash of Tabasco® sauce.

Hint: There are packages of instant hummus mix available in natural food and supermarket stores. Follow the directions on the package.

BLACK BEAN AND CORN MEXICAN FILLING

Mexican food for the salsa lovers—fill pita pockets or serve on a hot tortilla

**1 can (16 oz. [450 gm.]) black beans, drained and rinsed
1 can (15-16 oz. [425-50 gm.]) corn kernels, drained and rinsed
1 large tomato, chopped
1 avocado, peeled, seed removed, and chopped
½ cup (115 gm.) salsa
½ tsp. (2 gm.) ground cumin
2-3 sprigs of fresh cilantro leaves, chopped
1 tbsp. (15 ml.) lemon juice**

Combine all of the ingredients and stir to mix. Fill pita bread pockets. Serves 8.

Note: Do not add the avocado unless serving immediately.

BLACK BEAN FILLING

A complete protein meal with black beans and a staple

4-5 olive oil-marinated sun-dried tomatoes
¼ onion, chopped
½ green pepper, chopped
½ celery stalk, chopped
½ cup (115 gm.) leftover staple (bulgar wheat, rice, couscous)
1 can (15 oz. [425 gm.]) black beans, drained
1 tsp. (4 gm.) garam masala

In a skillet on medium-high heat, add the oil-marinated sun-dried tomatoes. Add the onion, green pepper, and celery and stir-fry for 5 minutes. Add the staple and black beans and stir for 2-3 minutes. Stir in the garam masala, and cook for 1 minute. Fills 4-5 pita pockets.

TOFU "EGGLESS" SANDWICH FILLING

The vegan, and individuals on a low cholesterol diet, can now enjoy a new twist to a traditional sandwich favorite. Spread the filling on hearty brown bread and top with lettuce, tomato, alfalfa sprouts, or any other favorite sandwich topping.

1 pkg. (14-16 oz. [400-450 gm.]) low-fat, firm tofu
¼ cup (60 gm.) imitation mayonnaise (suggestions below)
2 tsp. (8 gm.) prepared mustard
½ cup (60 gm.) pitted black olives, finely chopped (optional)
½ small onion, finely chopped
1 tsp. (15 ml.) lemon juice
2 tsp. (8 gm.) dill seed
1 tsp. (4 gm.) tumeric
Salt and pepper to taste

Rinse and drain the tofu well. In a small bowl, lightly mash the tofu with a fork. Stir in the remaining ingredients. Chill for 2-3 hours. Makes about 2 cups (450 gm.), enough for 6-8 sandwiches.

Suggestions for Imitation Mayonnaise

Best Foods *One Step* Salad Dressing®—It's found in most grocery stores. The main ingredients are soybean oil, vinegar, and vegetables (no eggs).

Nayonnaise®—It's found in natural food stores. The main ingredients are tofu and canola oil (no eggs).

Miracle Whip®—This is found in most grocery stores, is lower in cholesterol than mayonnaise, but does have egg whites as one of the ingredients.

EGG SALAD FILLING

A traditional favorite for pita bread or thick-sliced whole wheat bread

3 large hard-boiled eggs, peeled and chopped
3 tbsp. (45 ml.) mayonnaise
1 tsp. (4 gm.) prepared mustard
1 tbsp. (15 gm.) green relish or chopped pickle
Dash salt and pepper to taste

Mix all of the ingredients until well blended. Makes 3 sandwiches.

PIZZA, PIZZA, PIZZA

Everyone loves pizza. There are ready-made pizza shells available, like Boboli®, Trader Joe's Italian Herb Cheese Bread, or even English muffins cut in half. Here are some quick, easy, and fun pizza toppings to make pizza more loveable.

GARDEN VEGETABLE TOPPING

¼ cup (60 ml.) olive oil
⅓ cup (90 gm.) *each* of finely chopped carrots, celery, red onions, and mushrooms*
1 tsp. (4 gm.) salt
1 can (16 oz. [450 gm.]) Italian stewed tomatoes
1 large pizza shell or 2 medium-size shells
2 cups (500 ml.) mozzarella cheese, grated
½ tsp. (2 gm.) oregano

Preheat the oven to 450 degrees (232 degrees Celsius).

Heat the oil in a skillet and sauté the vegetables for 5 minutes. Add the salt and tomatoes. Simmer for 15 minutes, breaking up tomatoes while stirring. Spread the vegetable mixture on the pizza shell; sprinkle with cheese and oregano. Bake the pizza on a large baking sheet in the preheated oven for 12-15 minutes. Serves 3-5.

*Add or substitute other vegetables: green or red peppers, fresh tomatoes, broccoli, zucchini, etc.

BRIE AND SUN-DRIED TOMATOES

1 cup (225 gm.) pesto sauce, homemade or prepared
1 large pizza shell or 2 medium-size shells
½ lb. (225 gm.) Brie cheese, rind removed and cut
   into small cubes
½ cup (115 gm.) oil-marinated sun-dried tomatoes,
   drained and chopped

Preheat the oven to 450 degrees (232 degrees Celsius).

Spread the pesto sauce over the pizza shell. Evenly distribute the cheese and tomatoes over the top of the shell. Bake the pizza on a large baking sheet in the preheated oven for 12-14 minutes. Cut into slices. Serves 3-5.

SOUTH OF THE BORDER PIZZA

1 jar (12 oz. [340 gm.]) black bean dip
1 large pizza shell or 2 medium-size shells
½ cup (115 gm.) salsa
1 can (4 oz. [115 gm.]) green chili peppers, diced
1 tomato, chopped
½ cup (115 gm.) black olives, chopped
1 cup (225 gm.) Monterey Jack cheese, shredded

Preheat the oven to 450 degrees (232 degrees Celsius).

Spread the black bean dip evenly over the pizza shell. Spoon on the salsa, chili peppers, chopped tomato, and olives. Sprinkle with cheese. Bake the pizza on a large baking sheet in the preheated oven for 12-15 minutes. Serves 3-5.

Hint: Have guacamole and/or sour cream available for enhanced flavor.

YOGURT DIP

Serve with thick slices of whole wheat bread for a filling lunch.

1 cup (225 gm.) plain yogurt
1 tsp. (4 gm.) curry powder
1 tsp. (4 gm.) paprika
1 tsp. (4 gm.) ground cumin
½ tsp. (2 gm.) ground coriander

Combine the ingredients in a small container, mix well, and cover. Store in the refrigerator and until ready to transfer to an insulated lunch bag or box. Serves 1.

Note: Use Yogurt Dip for favorite raw vegetables such as cherry tomatoes, carrots, cucumbers, and zucchini.

VEGETABLES AND COUSCOUS

A combination of nutritious ingredients,
prepared in minutes, with a "thumbs up" on flavor.

1 tbsp. (15 gm.) canola oil
1 celery stalk, chopped
2 carrots, chopped
1 zucchini, sliced
1 medium-sized tomato, chopped
1 cup (250 ml.) water
1 cup (225 gm.) couscous
½ tsp. (2 gm.) dried mint
1 tsp. (4 gm.) parsley

In a medium-sized saucepan, heat the oil. Stir in the celery, carrots, zucchini, and tomatoes. Sauté the vegetables until tender, approximately 5 minutes. Add the water and bring to a boil. Stir in the couscous, mint, and parsley. Turn the heat off, cover, and let stand for 5 minutes. Serves 4-5.

Note: Nuts can be added for additional protein. You can prepare this recipe the night before for an away-from-home lunch the following day. Serve it either cold or reheated in a microwave oven.

PAPRIKA-SPICED NOODLES

*Prepare in minutes for an evening meal with
steamed vegetables and serve the leftovers for lunch.*

**1 pkg. (8 oz. [225 gm.]) egg noodles, cooked according to
package directions and drained**
1 tbsp. (15 gm.) butter
**1 can (10-11 oz. [285-310 gm.]) cream of mushroom soup,
stirred**
3 tsp. (15 gm.) paprika

In a microwave-safe bowl or casserole dish, stir together the cooked noodles, butter, mushroom soup, and paprika. Cook on high for 6 minutes in the microwave oven. Serves 4.

Hint: For variety, top with cheese, bread crumbs, or wheat germ.

FALAFEL QUICHE

*This recipe, entered with crabmeat instead of falafel,
was a finalist in the 1993 Wisconsin Milk Marketing Board Contest.*

3 eggs
1 cup (250 ml.) half & half
8 Falafel Balls, crumbled (see below)
1½ cups (340 gm.) Wisconsin cheddar cheese, shredded
1 stalk green onion, chopped
1 tbsp. (15 gm.) white wine Worcestershire sauce
¼ tsp. (1 gm.) salt
¼ tsp. (1 gm.) pepper
¼ tsp. (1 gm.) celery salt
½ tsp. (2 gm.) ground cayenne pepper
1 Pat-in-Pan Crust (see below)

Preheat the oven to 375 degrees (190 degrees Celsius.

Lightly beat the eggs and half & half together. Add the remaining ingredients and stir until well blended. Pour the pie filling into the prepared crust. Bake in the preheated oven for 40-45 minutes. Remove from oven and let stand 10 minutes. Serves 8.

FALAFEL BALLS

To prepare falafel balls: Mix 1 cup (225 gm.) falafel mix with ¾ cup (180 ml.) cold water. Let stand 10 minutes. Heat canola oil, at least 1 inch (2.5 cm.) deep, in a skillet. Roll the falafel mixture into ½-inch (1.25-cm.) balls; drop into hot oil and fry until golden brown. Remove and drain on paper towels. Refrigerate extra balls.

PAT-IN-PAN CRUST

2 cups (450 gm.) flour
2 tsp. (8 gm.) sugar
1 tsp. (4 gm.) salt
⅔ cup (160 ml.) canola oil
3 tbsp. (45 ml.) milk

In a mixing bowl, combine the flour, sugar, and salt. Add the oil and milk to the dry ingredients in the bowl and mix well. Evenly press the pie crust mixture into a 9-inch (22- to 23-cm.) pie pan, covering bottom and sides. Flute the edges.

QUICK LUNCH IDEAS

- Peanut butter spread on whole wheat bread
- Finely chopped walnuts mixed with cream cheese and spread on date nut bread
- Leftovers from dinner meals
- Soup prepared and frozen in individually sealed containers.
- Leftover cooked staples mixed with cooked or fresh vegetables. Add your favorite spice, such as curry, cayenne, oregano, or simply salt and pepper.

CHAPTER 6
Dinner

Today, families and individuals have so many extracurricular activities that it is difficult to have an enjoyable dinner meal together. The emphasis on "having a life" shouldn't mean flavorful and nutritional dinner meals are sacrificed. The recipes in this chapter are created for active people who want to enjoy time spent with family and friends but not be "chained" inside a kitchen.

SPICY STIR-FRY

*Use vegetables listed, store-packaged Chinese vegetables
(cleaned and cut), or other vegetables you have previously chopped*

**2 tbsp. (30 ml.) olive oil
1 carrot, chopped
½ onion, chopped
1 cup (225 gm.) *each* cauliflower florets and broccoli florets
1 cup (225 gm.) cabbage, shredded
½ tsp. (2 gm.) *each* cumin seed, curry powder, and garam masala**

Heat the olive oil on medium-high heat in a heavy skillet or wok. Toss in the vegetables, cumin seed, and curry and stir-fry for 5 minutes. Stir in the garam masala and stir-fry for 1 minute. Serves 2.

Hint: Serve over a bed of rice, kasha, or Chinese noodles.

VEGETABLE STIR-FRY

This basic stir-fry has endless variations.

**2½ tbsp. (37.5 ml.) peanut or sesame oil
½ head cabbage, shredded
1 green pepper, thinly sliced
1½ tbsp. (22.5 ml.) soy sauce
1 tsp. (4 gm.) sugar
1 can (4 oz. [115 gm.]) button mushrooms
Salt and pepper to taste
½ cup (125 ml.) water or wine**

Heat the oil in a wok, add cabbage, and stir-fry for 2-3 minutes. Add green pepper, soy sauce, sugar, and mushrooms. Season with salt and pepper. Pour the water in the wok, cover, and cook 5-7 minutes. Shake wok or stir a few times. Serves 4-6.

Variations: Substitute or add other ingredients, such as broccoli, carrots, celery, pea pods, string beans, water chestnuts, or tofu.

INDIAN VEGETABLES

The combination of vegetables, hot green chili, coconut,
and yogurt is a culinary experience.

¼ cup (60 ml.) canola oil
1 small onion, chopped
3 garlic cloves, minced
1 tbsp. (15 gm.) fresh gingerroot, grated
2 stalks carrots, sliced
1 pkg. (16 oz. [450 gm.]) frozen cut green beans
1 bunch (6-9) green onion stalks, sliced
2 green bell peppers, seeded and cut into strips
1 green jalapeno chili pepper, finely chopped
2 tbsp. (30 gm.) garam masala
1 cup (225 gm.) sweetened shredded coconut
1 cup (250 ml.) water
1 tsp. (4 gm.) salt
½ tsp. (2 gm.) pepper
1 cup (225 gm.) plain yogurt

Heat the oil in a wok or a large, heavy skillet on medium-high heat and sauté the onion, garlic, and ginger. Add the vegetables and stir-fry for 4-5 minutes. Add the garam masala, coconut, water, salt, and pepper and stir well. Bring to a boil, lower heat, and simmer for 15 minutes. Raise heat to high, add the yogurt, and cook for 2 minutes, stirring constantly. Serve over steamed rice. Serves 6-8.

TOFU/VEGETABLE STIR-FRY

Protein, vitamins, and minerals all in one delicious meal

TOFU/VEGETABLES

¼ cup (60 ml.) canola oil
1 pkg. (14-16 oz. [400-450 gm.]) tofu,
  cut into ½-inch (1.25-cm.) squares
2 cups (450 gm.) nappa cabbage, shredded
1 cup (225 gm.) bok choy, cut into thin slices
1 cup (225 gm.) cabbage
2 cups (450 gm.) broccoli spears
1 cup (225 gm.) onions, chopped
1 cup (225 gm.) green onions, chopped
2 carrots, shredded
1 cup (225 gm.) mushrooms, sliced
2 cups (450 gm.) snow peas

In a wok heat ½ inch (approximately ¼ cup [60 ml.]) canola oil. Add ⅓ of the tofu and stir-fry for 2 minutes on each side. Remove the tofu from the wok and let dry on a paper towel. Stir-fry the remaining tofu, ⅓ at a time. Stir-fry the nappa cabbage, bok choy, cabbage, broccoli, onions, and green onions for 3-4 minutes. Remove all of the cooked vegetables from the wok and place in a bowl. Place the carrots, mushrooms, and snow peas in the wok and stir-fry for 2-3 minutes. Return all the cooked vegetables and the tofu to the wok.

Add your choice of stir-fry sauce #1, #2, or #3 to the Tofu/Vegetable Stir-Fry in the wok and stir-fry for 2-3 minutes. Serve Tofu/Vegetable Stir-Fry over a bed of cooked rice, bulghur wheat, or Chinese noodles. Serves 5-6 people.

STIR-FRY SAUCE #1

½ tsp. (2 gm.) Dijon mustard
¼ cup (60 ml.) szechuan sauce
¼ cup (60 ml.) soy sauce
1 tsp. (5 gm.) gingerroot, grated
2 tbsp. (30 ml.) white cooking wine
2 tsp. (8 gm.) fresh cilantro, chopped fine

Place all of the ingredients in a blender or food processor and process on blend for one minute.

MANDARIN STIR-FRY SAUCE #2

1 cup (225 gm.) orange marmalade
2 tbsp. (30 ml.) soy sauce
2 tbsp. (30 ml.) white vinegar
2 tsp. (10 ml.) Chinese red pepper sauce or Tabasco® sauce
1½ tbsp. (20 gm.) cornstarch

In a small bowl mix all of the ingredients and stir until the cornstarch is dissolved.

STIR-FRY SAUCE #3

½ cup (125 ml.) soy sauce
½ cup (125 ml.) teriyaki sauce
Juice of ½ large lemon
1 tsp. (4 gm.) minced garlic

In a small bowl mix all of the ingredients until well blended.

Hint: Chop extra vegetables and store in the refrigerator for other recipes or quick snacks. Packaged stir-fry vegetables and prepared stir-fry sauces are available in supermarkets to reduce the preparation time.

TOFU AND PEA PODS

Gingerroot always adds zip to a recipe.

2 tsp. (8 gm.) cornstarch
1 tsp. (4 gm.) sugar
½ tsp. (2 gm.) salt
½ tsp. (2 gm.) pepper
2 tbsp. (30 ml.) soy sauce
¼ cup (60 ml.) water or wine
¼ cup (60 ml.) canola oil
1 pkg. (14-16 oz. [400-450 gm.]) tofu, cut
   into ½-inch (1.25-cm.) cubes
1 pkg. (16 oz. [450 gm.]) frozen pea pods, thawed*
1 can (8 oz. [225 gm.]) water chestnuts
1 tsp. (4 gm.) minced garlic or 1 clove garlic, grated
½ tsp. (2 gm.) minced gingerroot
   or 1 tsp. (4 gm.) gingerroot, grated

In a small bowl mix the cornstarch, sugar, salt, and pepper together. Stir in the soy sauce and water and set aside.

Heat the oil on medium-high heat in a wok or heavy skillet. Add the tofu, a few pieces at a time, and fry until golden brown. Remove the tofu and drain on a paper towel.

Stir-fry the pea pods, water chestnuts, garlic, and gingerroot for 2 minutes. Return the tofu to the wok and add the cornstarch-soy sauce mixture. Stir until the mixture coats the pea pods and water chestnuts; the mixture will be thick and bubbly. Serve with rice, noodles, or bulgur wheat. Serves 4.

*If a 16-oz. (450 gm.) package is not available, use two 10-oz. (285 gm.) packages.

GREEN BEANS, TOMATOES, AND TOFU #1

A combination Mediterranean and Oriental dish high in protein

1 pkg. (14-16 oz. [400-450 gm.) tofu,
   cut into ½-inch (1.25-cm.) cubes
1 can (16 oz. [450 gm.]) stewed tomatoes
2 pkgs. (10 oz. [285 gm.]) frozen green beans, defrosted
1 onion, chopped
1 clove garlic, minced
½ cup (125 ml.) vegetable broth or water
1 tsp. (4 gm.) dried mint or 1 tbsp. (15 gm.) fresh mint
2 tsp. (8 gm.) oregano
¼ tsp. (1 gm.) *each* salt and pepper

Put all of the ingredients in a large saucepan and bring to a boil. Reduce heat, cover, and simmer for 10 minutes. Serves 4-5.

GREEN BEANS, TOMATOES, AND TOFU #2

Indian spices for a different flavor
and a little easier to prepare than version #1

2 tbsp. (30 ml.) canola oil
1 pkg. (14-16 oz. [400-450 gm.]) firm tofu,
   cut into ½-inch (1.25-cm.) cubes
1 pkg. (10 oz. [285 gm.]) frozen green beans, thawed
1 jar (15 oz. [425 gm.]) Calcutta Masala Simmer Sauce
1 cup (250 ml.) water

Heat the oil in a heavy skillet. Add the tofu and stir-fry for 5-6 minutes. Add the green beans, Calcutta Masala Sauce, and water. Bring to a boil, reduce heat, and simmer for 8 minutes. Serves 4-5.

Note: Calcutta Masala Simmer Sauce is found in Eastern Indian, natural food stores, and the international section of supermarkets. If it is not available in your area, puree a can (16 oz. [450 gm.]) of stewed tomatoes with ½ tsp. (2 gm.) garam masala spice in a food processor or blender.

PEA PODS, RED PEPPERS, AND TOFU

Simply delicious!

2 tbsp. (30 gm.) sesame seeds
¼ cup (60 ml.) vegetable oil
1 pkg. (14-16 oz. [400-450 gm.]) firm tofu,
   cut into ½-inch (1.25-cm.) cubes
2 pkgs. (10 oz. [285 gm.] each) frozen Chinese pea pods,
   thawed and drained
1 large red bell pepper, thinly sliced and blanched
1 tsp. (5 ml.) sesame oil

In a small skillet, over medium heat, add the sesame seeds. Stir constantly until the seeds begin to brown. Remove to a small dish and set aside.

Heat 2 tbsp. (30 ml.) of the vegetable oil in a large skillet to medium heat. Add the tofu and stir constantly for 2-3 minutes. Add the pea pods and peppers, stirring constantly for 1 minute. Turn off the heat, stir in the sesame oil, and place the meal in a serving bowl. Sprinkle the toasted sesame seeds on top. Serves 4.

TOFU-BROCCOLI ORIENTAL

The spices of the Far East add zip to this dish.

¼ cup (60 ml.) soy sauce
2 tbsp. (30 ml.) sesame oil
¼ cup (60 ml.) lemon juice
1 pkg. (14-16 oz. [400- 450 gm.]) firm tofu,
   cut into 1-inch (2.5-cm.) pieces
1 tbsp. (15 gm.) cornstarch
2 tsp. (10 ml.) water
1 tbsp. (15 ml.) canola oil
2 medium onions, finely sliced
8 garlic cloves, minced
1 tbsp. (15 gm.) fresh gingerroot, grated
8 cups (3 large heads [900 gm.]) broccoli florets
¾ cup (180 ml.) vegetable broth
1 tbsp. (15 gm.) toasted sesame seeds

In a medium bowl whisk together the soy sauce, sesame oil, and lemon juice. Add the tofu and stir to coat with the marinade sauce. Set aside, stirring occasionally.

In a small bowl, blend the cornstarch and water until a smooth paste is formed. Set aside.

Heat the oil in a wok or large, heavy skillet. Add the onions and stir-fry for several minutes (onions should be translucent). Add the garlic, ginger, and broccoli and stir-fry for 1 minute. Pour in the tofu and marinade sauce. Cover the pan and steam for 2-3 minutes to tenderize the broccoli.

Add the cornstarch paste and vegetable broth and stir constantly until the liquid thickens. Toss on the sesame seeds and serve immediately over cooked rice or noodles. Serves 4.

TOFU-MUSHROOM ENCHILADAS

A good recipe to prepare ahead, freeze, and reheat

ENCHILADA SAUCE

1 can (15-16 oz. [425-450 gm.]) tomato sauce
1 cup (225 gm.) salsa
1 can (6 oz. [170 gm.]) green chilies
½ onion, finely chopped
2 garlic cloves, minced
1 tsp. (4 gm.) cumin seed, rubbed
¼ tsp. (1 gm.) cayenne pepper
½ tsp. (2 gm.) oregano

Preheat the oven to 350 degrees (177 degrees Celsius).

In large saucepan add all the sauce ingredients. Bring to a boil and simmer for 15-20 minutes. While sauce is simmering, prepare the enchiladas.

FILLING

1 pkg. (14-16 oz. [400-450 gm.]) firm tofu, broken up with a fork
1 cup (225 gm.) mushrooms, chopped fine
1 can (16 oz. [450 gm.]) black olives, chopped fine
1 dozen (burrito size) whole wheat flour tortillas
1 cup (225 gm.) salsa
1 cup (225 gm.) Monterey Jack cheese, grated (optional)

Mix together the tofu, mushrooms, and olives. Place ¼ cup (60 gm.) of filling in the center of a tortilla. Spoon 1 tbsp. (15 ml.) of sauce over the filling. Fold one long half of the tortilla over the filling. Tuck the opposite ends in towards the center and wrap the open half over the folded end. Place each tortilla, seam side down, in a lightly oiled 13-by-9-inch (32.5-by-22.5-cm.) baking dish.

Pour the remaining sauce over the enchiladas. Sprinkle the salsa and cheese over the top. Bake in the preheated oven for 20 minutes. Serves 8-12.

Note: There is a longer preparation time for this meal than others in this cookbook, but there's always plenty, too, for dinner guests or lunch the next day! To speed up the preparation of this recipe, use your favorite prepared canned enchilada sauce. To keep enchiladas juicy when reheating in the microwave, spread a small amount of salsa sauce over the tops of the enchiladas.

TOFU SPAGHETTI SAUCE

The Chinese were the originators of spaghetti noodles—
Tofu Spaghetti Sauce brings this meal full circle.

2 tbsp. (30 ml.) olive oil
1 onion, chopped
5 to 6 large mushrooms, sliced
2 cloves garlic, minced
1 pkg. (14-16 oz. [400-450 gm.]) tofu, mashed with a fork
1 can (15-16 oz. [425-450 gm.]) tomato sauce
1 can (8 oz. [225 gm.]) tomato paste
1 cup (250 ml.) vegetable broth
2 tsp. (8 gm.) Italian seasoning
1 bay leaf
⅛ tsp. (.5 gm.) cayenne pepper

In large, heavy skillet, in hot oil, sauté the onion, mushrooms, and garlic. Add the remaining ingredients. Bring to a boil, reduce heat, cover, and simmer for 30-45 minutes. Stir occasionally. Serve over cooked spaghetti noodles. Serves 4-6.

TOFU ITALIAN BALLS

Another version of a meatless meatball

1 pkg. (14-16 oz. [400-450 gm.]) tofu, mashed with a fork
2 eggs, lightly beaten
½ cup (115 gm.) bread crumbs
¼ cup (60 gm.) wheat germ
2 tbsp. (30 gm.) dehydrated onion flakes
1 tsp. (5 gm.) Italian seasoning
½ tsp. (2 gm.) salt
¼ tsp. (1 gm.) pepper
2 tbsp. (30 ml.) olive oil

In a large bowl mix all of the ingredients, except the olive oil. Shape into 1-inch balls. In a heavy skillet on medium-high heat, brown each ball in the oil. Drain on a paper towel. Makes 28 balls. Serve with your favorite sauce.

BOW-TIE ALFREDO

A new twist to Alfredo with a good source for protein and vitamins A and B

ALFREDO SAUCE

¼ lb. (115 gm.) ghee or butter
8 oz. (225 gm.) cream cheese
2 cups (500 ml.) evaporated skim milk
2 tbsp. (30 gm.) flour
½ tsp. (2 gm.) thyme
½ tsp. (2 gm.) basil
½ tsp. (2 gm.) fresh parsley

In a large skillet, preferrably cast iron, heat the butter on low heat until it has melted. Add the cream cheese and stir and cook for 2 minutes. Increase the heat to medium and add the milk. Simmer the sauce mixture for 2 minutes. Then add the flour and cook and stir frequently for 5 minutes. Add the spices and parsley, reduce heat to low, then simmer for 5 minutes. Stir occasionally.

VEGETABLES

1 tbsp. (15 ml.) olive oil
¾ cup (180 gm.) broccoli florets
2 cups (450 gm.) mushrooms, sliced
¼ cup (60 gm.) green peppers, chopped
¼ cup (60 gm.) red peppers, chopped
¼ cup (60 gm.) red onions, chopped
¼ cup (60 gm.) green onions, chopped

Heat the olive oil on medium for 1 minute. Sauté the vegetables for 3 minutes. Add the sautéed vegetables to the Alfredo Sauce and cook for 1 minute, stirring frequently.

BOW-TIE NOODLES

5 quarts (1.25 l.) water
Salt
1 pkg. (12 oz. [340 gm.]) bow-tie noodles
1 tbsp. (15 gm.) butter

In a large pot, bring the water and salt to a boil. Add the noodles and cook 5-6 minutes. Drain the noodles and place them in a large serving bowl. Add the butter and stir to coat them lightly to keep the noodles from sticking. Add the Alfredo Sauce and serve. Serves 6.

Time-saving tip: Boil the water for the noodles while chopping the vegetables. After pouring the cooked noodles into a strainer, use the same pan to prepare the vegetables. The total cooking time is 30 minutes.

ZITI AND BROCCOLI

A simple pasta dish that makes good use of broccoli stalks

1 pkg. (8 oz. [225 gm.]) ziti pasta
6 broccoli stalks, finely chopped
3 garlic cloves
¼ cup (60 ml.) olive oil
¼ cup (60 ml.) red wine
½ tsp. (2 gm.) basil
¼ tsp. (1 gm.) cayenne

In a large saucepan, cook the pasta according to package directions. Drain pasta.
While the pasta is cooking, in a large, heavy skillet, sauté the broccoli and garlic in olive oil for 5-6 minutes. Add the wine, basil, and cayenne. Stir and cook 1-2 minutes. Place the pasta in a large pasta dish. Top with the broccoli sauce. Serves 4.

NOODLES AND BROCCOLI

Adding a fresh vegetable to a packaged meal is super-fast nutrition.

    1½ cups (375 ml.) water
    ½ cup (125 ml.) milk
    1 tbsp. (15 gm.) butter or margarine
    1 pkg. (4.3 oz. [122 gm.]) Noodles & Sauce—a Lipton product
        usually located in the pasta section of supermarkets
    1 cup (225 gm.) fresh broccoli florets
    ¼ cup (60 gm.) almonds

In a medium saucepan, bring the water, milk, and butter to a boil. Stir in the noodle package contents and the broccoli. Continue boiling over medium heat, stirring occasionally, for 8 minutes. Let stand 2-3 minutes. Stir in the almonds. Serves 2.

Hint: A tossed green salad and a slice of hearty wheat bread will complete this meal.

CARAWAY CABBAGE AND APPLES

Cabbage is another cruciferous vegetable, helping to cleanse the intestinal tract and reduce the risk of colon cancer. Not only healthy, this dish is a diner's delight.

    1 tbsp. canola oil
    ½ head green cabbage, shredded
    2 large McIntosh or green apples, cored and chopped
    1 can (15 oz. [425 gm.]) kidney beans, drained
    1 tsp. (4 gm.) caraway seeds
    ¼ cup (60 gm.) plain yogurt or sour cream
    ½ cup (115 gm.) walnuts
    Salt and pepper to taste

Heat the oil in a large skillet over medium heat. Stir in cabbage, apples, kidney beans, and caraway. Cook about 8 minutes, stirring occasionally, until the cabbage is tender. Remove from heat and stir in the yogurt and walnuts. Season with salt and pepper. Serves 4.

ZUCCHINI AND TOMATO MEDLEY

This is the perfect accompaniment to pasta dishes.

¼ cup (60 ml.) olive oil
4 zucchini, sliced
1 large tomato, chopped
2 tsp. (8 gm.) Italian seasoning
¼ cup (60 gm.) Parmesan cheese, grated

Heat the oil on medium-high heat in a medium skillet. Stir in the zucchini, tomato, and seasoning. Sauté for 5-8 minutes. Add the Parmesan cheese, stirring for 1-2 minutes. Serves 4 as a side dish.

MARINARA SAUCE

Carrot is the Italian's secret ingredient to a sweet sauce.

2 cans (15-16 oz. [425-450 gm.]) tomato sauce
2 cans (14 oz. [435 ml.]) tomato paste
1 can (28 oz. [875 ml.]) whole tomatoes
1 carrot, grated fine
1 onion, chopped fine
4 garlic cloves, minced
2 tsp. (8 gm.) dill seed
2 tsp. (8 gm.) oregano
1 cup (250 ml.) water or ½ cup (125 ml.) water and ½ cup (125 ml.) wine (pour the water into the tomato sauce and paste cans to extract the juices)

In a large saucepan, add all of the ingredients. Cook for 8 minutes on medium heat, stirring every two minutes. Reduce heat to simmer and stir occasionally for two hours. This recipe allows for half of the sauce to be frozen and used at a later time for another pasta meal. Each half serves 6.

Tip: The sauce can also be cooked in a slow cooker or crock pot on low heat for 8-10 hours. This might be preferred because the sauce can be prepared in the morning before going to work; ready in the evening for dinner without having to watch over it. There's less mess—no stove or wall splashing of the marinara sauce!

WALNUT BALLS

A flavorful and healthy substitute for meat, with a chewy texture. Unlike artery-choking saturated fat in meat products, walnuts are predominately a polyunsaturated fat with high levels of linolenic acid and Omega-3 fatty acid, essential for the metabolism process.

1½ cups (340 gm.) walnuts
1 tsp. (5 gm.) garlic, crushed
½ onion, chopped
2 stalks green onion, chopped
¼ cup (60 gm.) celery, chopped
¼ tsp. (1 gm.) Italian seasoning
½ tsp. (2 gm.) salt
¼ tsp. (1 gm.) pepper
¼ cup (60 gm.) Parmesan cheese (optional)
2 eggs (or substitute ¼ cup [60 gm.] tofu)
6 slices whole wheat bread (crusts removed), crumbled
3 tbsp. (45 ml.) canola oil

Put the walnuts in a food processor or blender and process until finely chopped. Remove walnuts, place in a medium-sized bowl, and set aside. Add the vegetables to the processor or blender and process on chop. Place the chopped vegetables in the bowl with walnuts and add the spices, cheese, eggs, and bread crumbs. Mix the ingredients together until well blended. Shape the walnut-ball mixture into 1-inch (2.5-cm.) balls.

In a frying pan, add the canola oil and sauté the walnut balls until brown on all sides. Remove the walnut balls from the frying pan and place on a paper towel to drain.

Serve Walnut Balls in a Variety of Dishes

- Add to marinara sauce. Use your favorite prepared marinara sauce if time is restricted. Serve over cooked pasta or in a french roll.
- Place walnut balls in pita bread and top with chopped vegetables and salad dressing.
- Cut the walnut balls into small pieces and add to marinara sauce to be used in lasagna, or add to a rice mixture for stuffed peppers.
- Add to meatless recipes such as Thai-Spicy Noodles or Cauliflower Galore.
- Cream of Mushroom-Walnut Ball Casserole (recipe follows)
- Walnut Balls L'Orange (recipe follows)

CREAM OF MUSHROOM-WALNUT BALL CASSEROLE

1 recipe Walnut Balls
1 pkg. (8 oz. [225 gm.]) ribbon style pasta
2 cans (11-12 oz. [310-340 gm.]) cream of mushroom soup
1 cup (250 ml.) of milk
1 tsp. (4 gm.) basil
Dash pepper

Preheat the oven to 350 degrees (177 degrees Celsius).

Cook pasta according to package directions. Drain in colander and rinse twice in cold water. In a medium-sized saucepan, over medium heat, add the cream of mushroom soup, milk, basil, and pepper. Stir and cook until the sauce is hot.

Add the Walnut Balls and pasta. Stir to mix. Pour the mixture into a 9-by-7-inch (22.5-by-17.5-cm.) casserole dish. Bake in the preheated oven for 15 minutes.

WALNUT BALLS L'ORANGE

2 cups (500 ml.) water
1 cup (225 gm.) uncooked rice
1 recipe of Walnut Balls
3 cups (750 ml.) orange juice
2 tbsp. (30 ml.) brown sugar
1 orange with skin, sliced crosswise into thin slices*

In a saucepan, bring the water to a boil, add the rice, cover, reduce heat, and simmer for 25 minutes. If you haven't already, prepare the Walnut Balls as directed above. In the skillet used to cook the Walnut Balls, add the orange juice and brown sugar and stir for 1 minute. Bring the orange sauce just to boiling and reduce heat. Add the Walnut Balls and orange slices, cover, and simmer for 20 minutes. Serve Walnut Balls L'Orange over a bed of rice on a platter. Decorate with the orange slices and a few sprigs of parsley around the edge of the platter. Serves 4.

*The orange slices are very tasty.

Notes from Travis: When I was a child, Mom made this dish with pork chops. She told me one evening I had to learn how to cut my own pork chops. I didn't want to. This mild skirmish ended in a stalemate, and I chose not to eat that night. This was a tough decision for me because it was my favorite dish. Today, I still refuse to cut or eat meat, but I realized what I liked most about her recipe was the orange sauce.

FLASH PASTA

Pasta meals made in 15 minutes for people with hectic schedules

2 qt. (2 l.) water
Dash salt
½ package (8 oz. [225 gm.]) vermicelli or "angel hair" pasta

Bring the water and salt to a rapid boil. Add the vermicelli and stir frequently for 3-4 minutes. Drain, rinse with cold water, and drain again. Serves 2.

Hint: Vermicelli is extra-thin spaghetti and cooks in half the time of regular spaghetti. However, thicker sauces require wider pasta.

PASTA SAUCES

*Store in the cupboard or refrigerator/freezer either prepared
or homemade sauces. Heat prepared or homemade sauce in the microwave
oven. Follow the microwave manufacturer's recommended time.*

Marinara sauce. There are several ready-made marinara sauces available in supermarkets or natural food stores that use all natural ingredients without added sugar. There are several marinara sauce recipes here that can be prepared in advance, frozen, then reheated for a quick meal.

Pesto sauce. There are ready-made pesto sauces available in grocery stores that are quite delicious. The recipe later in this section takes approximately 15 minutes to prepare.

Flash pasta sauces follow (prepared in fifteen minutes while the pasta is cooking).

TOMATOES AND ONION SAUCE

*Always keep extra cans of tomatoes in the pantry
for a recipes that can be cooked in minutes*

2 tbsp. (30 ml.) olive oil
½ onion, chopped
1 can (28 oz. [800 gm.]) whole peeled tomatoes
2 tsp. (8 gm.) Italian seasoning
1 tbsp. (15 gm.) garlic, minced

Heat the olive oil in a medium-sized frying pan. Add the onion and sauté for 2 minutes. Add the tomatoes with the liquid. Add the seasoning and garlic and stir for 4-5 minutes, breaking up tomatoes with the side of a wooden spoon. Serves 6.

Ingredients to add for variety of flavor or additional nutrients:

- Red pepper flakes
- Leftover vegetables
- Sun-dried tomatoes
- Parmesan cheese
- Chopped red peppers
- Chopped mushrooms

CHERRY TOMATO-AND-MUSHROOM PASTA TOPPING

Children enjoy preparing this simple-to-make pasta topping

1 lb. (450 gm.) cherry tomatoes, cut in half
½ lb. (225 gm.) mushrooms, chopped
¼ cup (60 gm.) basil, chopped
4 cloves garlic
½ cup (115 gm.) bread crumbs
½ tsp. (2 gm.) salt
2 tbsp. (30 ml.) extra-virgin olive oil
½ cup (155 gm.) Parmesan or Romano cheese, grated (optional)

Preheat the oven to 350 degrees (177 degrees Celsius)

Place the tomatoes, mushrooms, basil, garlic, and bread crumbs on a baking sheet. Sprinkle salt and drizzle olive oil over the vegetable mixture. Bake in the preheated oven for 12-15 minutes. Toss the Cherry Tomato-and-Mushroom Pasta Topping with cooked pasta. Sprinkle with cheese. Serves 4-6.

VEGETABLE STOCK-TOMATO SAUCE

This sauce is also the right choice for reviving leftover pasta

1 cup (250 ml.) vegetable stock
2 medium tomatoes, chopped
½ onion, chopped
3-4 mushrooms, chopped
2 tbsp. (30 gm.) cilantro, chopped

In a small saucepan, bring the vegetable stock to a boil. Pour approximately ¼ cup (60 ml.) of the heated stock into a medium-size skillet. Add the vegetables and sauté for 5 minutes. Stir in the remaining vegetable stock and cilantro. In a large bowl, add the Vegetable Stock-Tomato Sauce to 8 oz. of cooked pasta. Toss sauce and pasta together. Serves 4.

WILD MUSHROOM TOPPING

More and more supermarkets are stocking wild mushrooms.
If they are not easily found, use the white mushrooms.

¼ cup (60 ml.) red wine
1 lb. (450 gm.) wild mushrooms, sliced
Salt and pepper
1 medium onion, chopped
2 garlic cloves, minced
2 tsp. (8 gm.) basil

In a skillet, heat 2 tbsp. (30 ml.) of the wine and add the mushrooms. Sauté the mushrooms until they are golden brown. Sprinkle with salt and pepper. Remove from the skillet and set aside in a bowl. Add the remaining wine to the skillet, add the onion and garlic, and cook on high heat for 2 minutes. Return the sautéed mushrooms to the skillet. Add the basil and cook, stirring constantly, for 1 minute. Serve on top of cooked pasta or pizza. Serves 4.

TUSCAN PASTA SAUCE

Plain in style, like Tuscan architecture, but a classic recipe favorite

¼ cup (60 ml.) virgin olive oil
2 tsp. (8 gm.) minced garlic
¼ tsp. (1 gm.) crushed red chili flakes

Mix ingredients in a small microwave-safe glass bowl. Heat in a microwave oven on high for 2 minutes. Let stand a few minutes before pouring over hot pasta. Serves 4.

Note: For small-size pasta, prepare 2 cups (450 gm.) of pasta; for large-size pasta, prepare 3 cups (675 gm.) according to package directions.

CREAMY PASTA SAUCE

Nutmeg and pepper are the flavor enhancers for this pasta sauce.
Serve this dish with a tossed green salad.

2 cups (500 ml.) whole milk
2 tbsp. (30 gm.) butter
4 tsp. (16 gm.) unbleached white flour
¼ tsp. (1 gm.) salt
½ tsp. (2 gm.) pepper
¼ tsp. (1 gm.) nutmeg
½ cup (115 gm.) almonds

In a medium saucepan on medium heat, scald the milk and bring just to a boil. Place the butter in a small bowl and heat in the microwave oven on high for 60 seconds. Add the flour and whisk for 1 minute. Add the scalded milk and spices and whisk the sauce together for 30-60 seconds. Place the bowl in the microwave oven and heat on high for 1½ minutes. Whisk again for 1 minute. After serving prepared pasta in individual bowls, top with Creamy Pasta Sauce and sprinkle with almonds. Serves 6.

PESTO FOR PASTA

For the purist who wants homemade, traditional pesto sauce

½ bunch fresh basil
½ bunch fresh parsley leaves
¼ cup (60 gm.) pine nuts, toasted*
2 tbsp. (30 gm.) grated Romano cheese
2 garlic cloves
¼ tsp. (1 gm.) *each* of salt and pepper
½ cup (125 ml.) olive oil

Place all of the ingredients, except the olive oil, in a food processor or blender and finely chop. While processing, add the olive oil and blend until the pesto is smooth. Store in a tightly sealed jar in the refrigerator. Makes about 1 cup (250 ml.).

*To toast the pine nuts, heat in a heavy, small skillet over medium-high heat, stirring constantly for approximately 4 minutes. The toasted pine nuts will be a light golden brown color.

SPINACH PESTO SAUCE

Another favorite version of a pesto sauce

¼ cup (60 gm.) pine nuts, toasted
½ bunch spinach leaves
½ bunch basil leaves
1 cup (225 gm.) grated Parmesan cheese
2 garlic cloves
½ tsp. (2 gm.) salt
¼ tsp. (1 gm.) pepper
1 cup (250 ml.) olive oil

Place all of the ingredients, except the olive oil, in a food processor or blender. Blend until all of the ingredients are finely chopped. Add the oil and blend until smooth. Transfer to a glass jar or small bowl and cover with an airtight lid or plastic wrap until ready to serve. Makes about 1½ cups (750 ml.).

BROCCOLI-PINE NUT PESTO SAUCE

Another dish Travis created that his friends believe,because
of the delicious flavor, must take hours to prepare.

½ cup (125 ml.) olive oil
4 garlic cloves, minced
¼ cup (60 gm.) pine nuts
4-5 stalks broccoli, chopped
¼ tsp. (1 gm.) dried basil

Heat the olive oil in a large skillet and sauté the garlic cloves for 3-4 minutes. Add the pine nuts and stir for 1 minute. Add the broccoli and basil and sauté until the broccoli becomes bright green and slightly crispy, approximately 5-6 minutes. Serve over cooked pasta noodles. Serves 4.

RIGATONI PASTA

The pasta fun never ends!

Water
1 pkg. (1 lb. [450 gm.]) rigatoni pasta
2 tbsp. (30 ml.) olive oil
1 garlic clove, minced
1 bunch broccoli, chopped
1 can (15-16 oz. [425-450 gm.]) cannellini beans, drained
¼ cup (60 gm.) oil-marinated sun-dried tomatoes, drained
1½ cup (125 ml.) vegetable broth
Salt and pepper to taste
¼ cup (60 gm.) Parmesan cheese, grated

In a large saucepan of boiling water, cook the pasta according to package directions. While the pasta is cooking, heat the olive oil on medium heat in a large skillet. Add the garlic and sauté for 2 minutes. Stir in the broccoli, reduce heat, cover, and cook 3 minutes. Drain the pasta, rinse in cold water, drain again, and put in a large bowl. Add the beans, tomatoes, broth, and spices to the sautéed broccoli. Simmer uncovered for 5 minutes. Add the drained pasta and toss. Sprinkle with cheese. Serves 5-6.

VEGETABLE MEDLEY LASAGNA

A classic meal so healthy and yummy

1 pkg. (16 oz. [450 gm.]) wide noodles
3 tbsp. (45 ml.) olive oil (for sautéing vegetables, cooking the noodles, and coating the baking pan)
1 green pepper, sliced
2 zucchini, sliced
1 onion, chopped
1 lb. (450 gm.) mozzarella cheese, sliced thin or packaged already shredded
8 oz. (225 gm.) ricotta cheese
1 egg, lightly beat the egg with a fork and stir into the ricotta cheese
1 cup (225 gm.) Parmesan cheese, grated
4 cups (900 gm./1 l.) Marinara Sauce (Use half of the Marinara Sauce recipe, or your favorite prepared marinara sauce.)

Preheat the oven to 375 degrees (190 degrees Celsius).

Cook the noodles according to package directions. While the noodles are cooking, prepare the vegetables. Heat 1 tbsp. (15 ml.) of the olive oil in a skillet. Add the vegetables and sauté for 4-5 minutes. Drain the noodles and stir in 1 tbsp. (15 ml.) olive oil to keep them from sticking.

Lightly oil the bottom of a 13-by-9-by-2-inch (32.5-by-22.5-by-5-cm.) baking pan. Build the lasagna in layers as follows:

—A single layer of cooked noodles to cover the bottom of the pan.
—A single layer of sautéed vegetables
—A single layer of marinara sauce
—A single layer of mozzarella, ricotta, then Parmesan cheese

Repeat the above for the second layer. The third layer will be noodles, mozzarella cheese, and the top sprinkled with Parmesan cheese.

Bake in the preheated oven for 30-35 minutes. While the lasagna is baking, clean the pans, and take a refreshing shower! Serves 8-10.

Hint: If there are extra cooked lasagna noodles, cut up into small pieces. In a bowl add the noodles, stir in a small amount of melted butter or olive oil, sprinkle with Parmesan cheese, and refrigerate. The noodles, leftover cooked vegetables, and vegetable broth can later be combined and heated in the microwave oven for a quick-fix lunch or snack.

PASTA PRIMAVERA

Another "made-in-America" recipe, made even easier to prepare

1 pkg. (1 lb. [450 gm.]) linguini
1 pkg. (10 oz. [285 gm.]) frozen mixed
  or Italian-style vegetables
1 pkg. (10 oz. [285 gm.]) frozen chopped broccoli
½ tsp. (2 gm.) basil
¼ cup (60 ml.) olive oil*
¼ cup (60 gm.) pine nuts, toasted
¼ cup (60 gm.) Parmesan cheese, grated (optional)

Cook linguini according to package directions. Add the frozen vegetables to the boiling linguini water several minutes before the linguini is done. Drain the pasta and vegetables and toss with olive oil. Sprinkle with pine nuts and cheese. Serves 4.

*You can substitute an olive oil with added herbs such as basil, or other oils such as walnut oil.

AVOCADO AND GARBANZO BEAN PASTA

Alone, avocados are bland.
Blended with other foods and spices, avocados become addictive.

1 pkg. (1 lb. [450 gm.]) spaghetti
3 large ripe avocados, peeled, pitted, and mashed
3 tbsp. (45 ml.) lemon or lime juice
½ cup (115 gm.) salsa
½ tsp. (2 gm.) garlic, minced
1 tsp. (4 gm.) salt
1 small can (8-9 oz. [225-255 gm.]) garbanzo beans, drained
4 cherry tomatoes, quartered

Cook the spaghetti, drain, and put in a bowl. Mash the avocados together with lemon juice, salsa, garlic, and salt. Add the garbanzo beans and mix. Add the avocado mix to the spaghetti and lightly toss. Garnish each dish with tomatoes. Serves 4.

SPINACH LASAGNA

A favorite meal for vegetarians and nonvegetarians

1 tbsp. (15 ml.) olive oil
2 cups (450 gm.) fresh mushrooms, sliced
1 cup (225 gm.) grated carrot
½ onion, chopped
1 can (15-16 oz. [425-450 gm.]) tomato sauce
1 can (6 oz. [170 gm.]) tomato paste
½ cup (115 gm.) olives, chopped
1½ tsp. (6 gm.) oregano
1 tsp. (4 gm.) garlic, minced
10 lasagna noodles
1 lb. (450 gm.) spinach,* leaves cleaned
2 cups (450 gm.) cottage cheese
1 lb. (450 gm.) Monterey Jack cheese, sliced
1 cup (225 gm.) Parmesan cheese, grated
1 tsp. (4 gm.) Italian seasoning (optional)

Preheat the oven to 375 degrees (190 degrees Celsius).

In a saucepan, cook the mushrooms, carrots, and onion in the oil until tender (5-6 minutes). Stir in the tomato sauce, tomato paste, olives, oregano, and garlic. Heat on high until just boiling, then lower heat and simmer for 15-20 minutes. While the sauce is cooking, prepare the noodles.

Cook the noodles in boiling water for 8-10 minutes. Drain and rinse in cold water to keep them from sticking. While the water is boiling, prepare the spinach.

In a saucepan add just enough water so that it clings to the spinach leaves. Cover the pan and steam for 3-5 minutes. Drain spinach.

In a greased 13-by-9-by-2-inch (32.5-by-22.5-by-5-cm.) baking dish, layer half of the noodles, cottage cheese, spinach, Monterey Jack cheese, and vegetable-marinara sauce. Repeat layers using Monterey Jack cheese as the last layer. Sprinkle with Parmesan cheese and Italian seasoning. Bake in the preheated oven for 30 minutes and let stand for 10 minutes before serving. Serves 8-10.

*If desired, substitute 2 pkgs. (10 oz. [285 gm.]) frozen spinach, thawed and drained.

Hint: Although the preparation time is approximately 30 minutes and the baking time is also 30 minutes, the lasagna can be prepared, baked, frozen, and reheated for serving guests. When guests arrive, your kitchen will be clean and you'll be able to enjoy them rather than be stuck in the kitchen.

POTATO CASSEROLE

*This recipe, for potato aficionadas, makes good use
of the modern convenience of frozen potatoes,
cleaned, cut, and ready to oven-bake.*

1 pkg. (24 oz. [675 gm.]) frozen potato wedges with skin
2 tsp. (8 gm.) garlic, minced
5-6 oil-marinated sun-dried tomatoes, quartered
2 carrots, cut into ½-inch (1.25-cm.) slices
1 tsp. (4 gm.) red pepper flakes
¼ cup (60 ml.) olive oil
1 tsp. (4 gm.) oregano
½ tsp. (2 gm.) salt
Parmesan cheese

Preheat the oven to 450 degrees (232 degrees Celsius).

In a large bowl, mix all of the ingredients. Spread the mixture in a 13-by-9-by-2-inch (32.5-by-22.5-by-5-cm.) baking pan. Bake for 20-25 minutes in the preheated oven. Sprinkle with Parmesan cheese, if desired. Serves 5-6.

NUTTY LOAF

*Walnuts, bread crumbs, and oatmeal are substituted
for the ground meat without any loss of flavor.*

1½ cups (340 gm.) walnuts, ground
1½ cups (340 gm.) bread crumbs
¼ cup (60 gm.) oatmeal or substitute with wheat germ
2 eggs, beaten
¼ onion, finely chopped
¼ cup (60 gm.) Parmesan cheese, grated
¼ cup (60 ml.) milk
½ tsp. (2 gm.) sage
1 tsp. (5 gm.) salt
¼ tsp. (1 gm.) pepper
¼ cup (60 ml.) ketchup

Preheat the oven to 350 degrees (177 degrees Celsius).

Combine all of the ingredients, except the ketchup. Shape into a loaf and place in a lightly oiled loaf pan. Spread the ketchup over the top of the loaf. Bake in the preheated oven for 1 hour. Serves 4.

Variations: Mix in ½ a carrot, grated; cut rings of green bell pepper and press into the top of the loaf; omit ketchup and serve with prepared mushroom gravy or Cranberry Salsa (see recipe).

Hint: Scrub some potatoes, white and/or sweet, and bake with the Nutty Loaf. Baked potatoes are great-tasting, very nutritious, and easy to prepare.

WALNUT PATTIES

Another flavorful meatless hamburger

2 eggs, beaten
1 cup (225 gm) walnuts, finely chopped
1 cup (225 gm.) oatmeal
3 tbsp. (45 ml.) milk
½ onion, finely chopped
1 tbsp. (15 ml.) A.1.® Steak Sauce
Pinch salt and pepper
2 tbsp. (30 ml.) canola oil
½ cup (125 ml.) water
5-6 mushrooms

Mix the eggs, walnuts, oatmeal, milk, onion, A.1.® Steak Sauce, salt, and pepper. Form into 6 patties. Heat the oil on medium-high in a heavy skillet. Add the patties and brown on both sides. Add the water and mushrooms to the skillet. Reduce heat to low, cover, and simmer for 8-10 minutes. The water will evaporate. Serve on buns or kaiser rolls. Serves 4-6.

SLOPPY JOES SANS HAMBURGER

TVP® replaces the chewy texture of meat in these Sloppy Joes,
and in recipes like chili, hash, enchiladas, etc.

1 cup (250 ml.) boiling water
1 cup (225 gm.) TVP®
2 tbsp. (30 ml.) canola oil
1 medium bell pepper, chopped
1 onion, chopped
1 can (15-16 oz. [425-450 gm.]) Sloppy Joe sauce*
¼ cup (60 gm.) yellow corn kernels
¼ cup (60 ml.) water

Bring the water to a boil in a saucepan. Add the TVP®, stir, cover, and set aside. Heat the oil in a heavy skillet over medium-high heat; sauté the pepper and onion for 5-6 minutes. Add the TVP®, Sloppy Joe sauce, and corn. Swish the Sloppy Joe can with the ¼ cup (60 ml.) water to clean out the sauce from the can and pour into the skillet. Cook for 3-5 minutes until heated through. Serve on rolls, toast, or in pita pockets. Serves 4-6.

*Or you can substitute a Sloppy Joe dry mix, fixing as directed on the package. If neither Sloppy Joe sauce or dry mix are available, bring 1 15-16 oz. (425-450 gm.) can tomato sauce, ½ finely chopped onion, and 1 tsp. (4 gm.) garlic powder to a boil. Reduce heat and simmer for 30-35 minutes.

VEGGIE BURGER DRESSINGS

The most popular fast-food restaurant burgers are often popularized not because of the meat, but because of their "secret sauce" recipes. Cook your favorite Veggie Burger (see the Walnut Burger recipe) or use a prepared one, such as Boca Burger®, Green Giant Harvest Burger®, or Morningstar Farms Garden Meatless Vege Patties®. Choose one of the "secret sauce" recipes and enjoy an American legend reborn.

TANGY THOUSAND ISLAND DRESSING

½ cup (125 ml.) bottled Thousand Island dressing
1 tsp. (4 gm.) prepared horseradish
Dash Tabasco® sauce

Mix ingredients until well blended; refrigerate until ready to spread on a bun. Makes ½ cup (125 ml.), enough for 4 patties.

COUNTRY STYLE DRESSING

½ cup (125 ml.) bottled Ranch® dressing
2 tbsp. (30 gm.) relish
½ tsp. (2 gm.) ground cumin

Mix ingredients until well blended; refrigerate until ready to spread on a bun. Makes ½ cup (125 ml.), enough for 4 patties.

MUSHROOM-WORCESTERSHIRE DRESSING

1 can (4 oz. [115 gm.]) sliced mushrooms, drained
½ cup (125 ml.) water
1 vegetable bouillon cube
1 tbsp. (15 ml.) Worcestershire sauce
1 tsp. (4 gm.) cornstarch
2 tbsp. (30 ml.) water

In a medium skillet, on medium-high heat, stir the mushrooms, water, bouillon, and Worcestershire sauce. Mix the cornstarch and 2 tbsp. (30 ml.) water to make a smooth paste. Pour cornstarch paste into the skillet and stir until the mixture is thick and bubbly. Makes ¾ cup (187.5 ml.), enough for 4 patties.

*Substitute with A.1.® Steak Sauce if vegetarian Worcestershire sauce is unavailable.

WALNUT-POTATO HASH

For many people converting to a vegetarian diet is easy,
except they yearn for hash. Weep no more—this hash is delicious!

2 tbsp. (30 ml.) canola oil
¼ cup (60 gm.) onion, chopped
6 potatoes, scrubbed clean and chopped
2 tbsp. (30 gm.) peanut butter
1 cup (250 ml.) milk
2 stalks celery, finely chopped
1 cup (225 gm.) walnuts, broken into pieces
1 green pepper, finely chopped

Heat the oil in a large, heavy skillet on medium-high heat; add the onion and potatoes. Pan-fry for 5 minutes. Add the peanut butter and milk; stir and bring to a boil. Add the remaining ingredients. Turn the heat down to low and cook for 30 minutes; stir occasionally. Serves 4-5.

CAULIFLOWER GALORE

Prepared in minutes and high in Vitamin K

1 cauliflower, cleaned and cut into flowerets
1 can (10-11 oz. [285-310 gm.]) condensed cream
   of asparagus soup
1 tsp. (5 ml.) lemon juice
⅛ tsp. (.5 gm.) nutmeg

Steam the cauliflower for 5 minutes. Drain and place the cauliflower in a serving bowl. Combine the soup, lemon juice, and nutmeg. Heat just until the soup begins to bubble. Pour the heated soup over the cauliflower. Serves 4-5.

Hint: To vary the flavor, use ½ tsp. (2 gm.) curry powder instead of the lemon juice and nutmeg, or use cream of broccoli soup with a ¼ tsp. (1 gm.) garlic powder. The Walnut Balls can be added (heat with the soup) for texture and to enrich the meal with protein and vitamins B3 and B6.

MEDITERRANEAN BURRITOS

Made in just under 20 minutes and are squash full of vitamin A

3 tbsp. (45 ml.) olive oil
4 or 5 medium yellow squash, thinly sliced
½ cup (115 gm.) of onion, chopped
⅓ cup (90 gm.) green onions, chopped
⅓ can (14-15 oz. [400-425 gm.]) whole stewed tomatoes,
   chopped fine
2 tbsp. (30 ml.) juice from can of stewed tomatoes
1 tsp. (2 mg.) oregano
1 tsp. (2 mg.) basil
8 large-size flour tortillas
1½ cups (340 gm.) cheddar cheese

Heat the olive oil in a skillet over medium-high heat for one minute. Add the yellow squash and stir-fry for 4-5 minutes until squash is *al dente*. Add the onions and stir for 1-2 minutes. Add the tomatoes with juice, oregano, and basil and stir for 1-2 minutes. Turn the burner off.

Heat each tortilla on top of a burner, both sides for 30 seconds, or place them all in a microwave container, cover with a paper towel, and microwave for 20-30 seconds.

Spoon out a small portion of the squash mixture into each tortilla and sprinkle with several tablespoons of cheddar cheese. Roll the tortilla like an enchilada (see the Tofu-Mushroom Enchiladas recipe for instructions). Serves 6-8.

Tip: Leftover Mediterranean Burritos should be placed in a microwave-safe container and refrigerated or frozen until ready to reheat. When ready to reheat, top the burritos with a small amount of salsa and/or cheese, cover, and reheat according to the microwave oven's manufacturer's recommended instructions.

Time and money-saving tip: Use the remaining portion of stewed tomatoes to make salsa (see the Tomato Salsa recipe).

BLACK BEAN AND RICE BURRITOS

A south-of-the-border favorite

1 can (15 oz. [425 gm.]) black beans, undrained
2 stalks green onion, chopped
1/3 cup (90 gm.) salsa
1/4 tsp. (1 gm.) *each* cumin and chili powder
1 cup (225 gm) cooked "leftover" rice
6 large-size flour tortillas
1/4 cup (60 gm.) sour cream or plain yogurt (optional)

Cook the black beans, green onions, salsa, and spices in a saucepan over medium-high heat; bring to a boil. Lower the heat and simmer 5-6 minutes. Stir in the rice and cook for 1 minute. Remove from heat.

Cover and heat the tortillas in the microwave for 40-60 seconds. Then spoon approximately 1/3 cup (90 mg.) of the bean-rice mixture in the center of each tortilla. Add a dollop of sour cream and roll up. Serves 6.

Hint: Use this recipe for nachos or tortillas. Top with chopped cabbage or lettuce and tomatoes. Garnish with your favorite toppings: guacamole, cheese, salsa, chili sauce, and/or sliced olives.

REFRIED BEAN BURRITO

Prepare in minutes for delicious fast food.

1 can (16 oz. [450 gm.]) vegetarian refried beans
6-8 large-size flour tortillas

In a medium skillet over medium heat, bring refried beans to just bubbling while stirring continually. Heat the tortillas on an open flame or warm in the microwave. Spoon the refried beans in the center of each tortilla and roll up. Serves 4-6.

Variations (add to the basic Refried Bean Burrito):

- Leftover rice (beans and rice together are a complete protein); cook with the refried beans
- Potatoes, chopped and cooked before adding to the refried beans
- Chopped tomatoes
- Grated cheese
- Sour cream
- Salsa
- Guacamole

STOVETOP ENCHILADAS

This recipe will tantalize tongues longing for a tangy treat.

8 large-size flour tortillas
2 cups (450 gm.) finely chopped kale
4 scallions, finely chopped
½ cup (115 gm.) black olives, chopped
2 cups (450 gm.) Jack cheese, shredded
**¼ cup (60 ml.) canola oil or substitute with ¼ cup (60 ml.)
   vegetable broth**
1 can (16 oz. [450 gm.]) enchilada sauce
½ cup (115 gm.) minced fresh cilantro

Lay out each tortilla. Divide the kale, scallions, olives, and cheese into equal amounts and sprinkle on each tortilla. Roll up each tortilla as directed in the Tofu-Mushroom Enchiladas recipe. Heat the oil in a large skillet over medium-high heat. Place each enchilada, seam-side-down, in the skillet. Pour the enchilada sauce over the enchiladas, bring to a boil, cover, reduce heat, and simmer for 7-8 minutes. Sprinkle with cilantro. Serves 6-8.

VEGETABLE CHOW MEIN

It's simple to make and delicious to eat.

2 tbsp. (30 ml.) canola oil
2 tbsp. (30 ml.) sesame oil
3-4 carrots, sliced
3-4 stalks bok choy, chopped
3 stalks celery, chopped
½ head cabbage, shredded
8-10 mushrooms, sliced
½ lb. (225 gm.) broccoli, cut into florets
1 jalapeno pepper, chopped
2 tbsp. (30 gm.) gingerroot, peeled and minced, or substitute
   with 1 tsp. (5 ml.) prepared ginger
2 cloves garlic, minced
¼ cup (60 gm.) flour
1 cup (250 ml.) whole milk
2 tbsp. (30 gm.) vegetable soup and dip mix (usually located in
   the soup and bouillon section of the supermarket)
2 cups (500 ml.) water
¼ cup (60 ml.) soy sauce
Cooked rice

Heat the canola and sesame oils in a wok or large, heavy skillet. Add the vegetables, gingerroot, and garlic and stir-fry for 5-6 minutes. Turn the heat off. Add the flour to the milk and mix together briskly with a fork or handmixer. Stir in the vegetable soup and dip mix and let the milk mixture sit for several minutes. Turn the heat back on under the vegetables and pour the milk mixture over the vegetables. Cook on medium-high for 1-2 minutes. Add the water and soy sauce to the cooked vegetables and stir for 2 minutes. Serve on a bed of cooked rice. Serves 8.

Hint: Chopping the vegetables is the most time-consuming procedure for this dish. So, it's a good time to chop extra amounts of the vegetables to be stored in the refrigerator or to use immediately in another recipe. For instance, the second half of the cabbage head can be used for coleslaw or placed in a crock pot to make a vegetable soup. Even with all the chopping and slicing, this meal can be prepared in less than 30 minutes. If you hate chopping, use 2 packages of stir-fry vegetables purchased from natural food stores or supermarkets.

SOBA

This is Travis's version (which includes extra pasta) of a favorite Japanese dish he prepared as a sushi chef. The tamari (Japanese sauce) and the soba noodles can be found in most natural food stores, as well as the international section in many supermarkets.

1 tsp. (5 ml.) sesame oil
¾ cup (180 ml.) water
¼ cup (60 ml.) tamari sauce
2 cups (450 gm.) cabbage, shredded
1 zucchini, sliced into ¼-inch (.65-cm.) chunks
5 fresh shittake mushrooms*
¼ cup (60 gm.) green onions, chopped
1 carrot, peeled into strips
1 pkg. (8-9 oz. [225-255 gm.]) soba noodles, cooked** and drained

Heat the oil in a large skillet on high heat. Add the water and tamari sauce and heat just to a boil. Add the cabbage and zucchini, stir, and cook for 2-3 minutes. Add the mushrooms, green onions, and carrot; stir; and cook for 4-5 minutes. Add the soba noodles and stir to separate the noodles. Serves 4.

*If fresh shittake mushrooms are not available, soak dry shittake mushrooms according to package directions.

**Cook slightly under the package instruction time; for example, if cooking time is 8 minutes, cook 6 minutes.

THAI-SPICY NOODLES

Lots of zip to a vegetable and pasta dish

1 tbsp. (15 ml.) sesame oil
1 lb. (450 gm.) fresh broccoli, trimmed into florets
4 carrots, sliced
1 onion, sliced
1 jalapeno pepper, chopped
4 cloves garlic, minced
1 cup (250 ml.) vegetable broth
1 tbsp. (15 gm.) basil, crushed
1 tbsp. (15 ml.) Worcestershire sauce or A.1.® Steak Sauce
Juice of 1 lemon
1 pkg. (8 oz. [225 gm.]) narrow noodles, cooked according to
   the directions on the package and drained.

Heat the oil in a wok or large, heavy skillet. Add the broccoli, carrots, onion, pepper, and garlic and stir-fry for 5-6 minutes. Add the broth, basil, Worcestershire sauce, and stir-fry for 1-2 minutes. Pour in the lemon juice, stir, and serve over the cooked noodles. Serves 6.

EGG FOO YONG

Prepare extra for a special lunch treat the next day.

1 green pepper
1 onion
¼ cup (60 ml.) red wine
2 cups (450 gm.) fresh bean sprouts
6 eggs (you can use just the egg whites)
¼ tsp. (1 gm.) salt
¼ tsp. (1 gm.) pepper
1 can (8 oz. [225 gm.]) water chestnuts, grated
Canola oil

Grate the green pepper and onion in a blender or food processor. Heat the wine in a large skillet on medium-high heat and add the bean sprouts, green pepper, and onion. Sauté until the onions are translucent (approximately 5 minutes). Place the sautéed vegetables in a bowl. Put the eggs, salt, and pepper in the blender or processor. Process until frothy. Put the water chestnuts in the blender with the eggs and grate for 1 cycle. Add the egg-water chestnut mixture to the vegetables and mix well. Pour the oil, to the depth of ⅛ inch (.32 cm.), in the bottom of the skillet and heat on medium-high. Pour the Egg Foo Yong mixture into the skillet, about ⅓ cup (80 ml.) for each cake, and brown on both sides like a pancake. Remove the cakes and place on a paper towel to drain. While the cakes are browning, prepare the Egg Foo Yong Soy Sauce.

EGG FOO YONG SOY SAUCE

2 cups (500 ml.) vegetable broth or water
¼ cup (60 ml.) soy sauce
2 tbsp. (30 gm.) cornstarch

Put all of the Soy Sauce ingredients in the blender and process on medium speed until smooth. Pour the Soy Sauce in the skillet and cook on medium-high until the sauce is clear. Return the cakes to the skillet and spoon the Egg Foo Yong Soy Sauce over them, cover, lower the heat, and heat the cakes for 1 minute. Serves 6.

SAUTEED VEGETABLES AND TAHINI

Combine this meal with a staple for a
meal high in Vitamin E and "complete" protein.

2 tbsp. (30 ml.) canola oil
½ onion, chopped
2 unpared zucchini squash, cut into quarters
3 tomatoes, cut into wedges
1 can (3 oz. [85 gm.]) sliced mushrooms
¼ tsp. (1 gm.) salt
¼ tsp. (1 gm.) curry powder
¼ tsp. (1 gm.) ginger
Pepper to taste
½ cup (115 gm./125 ml.) Tahini Sauce

Heat the oil on medium-high heat in a medium-sized skillet and add the onion and zucchini. Cover, reduce the heat to medium, and cook the vegetables for 5 minutes. Add the remaining ingredients, except the Tahini Sauce, and cook for 5 more minutes. Stir in the Tahini Sauce and cook 1 minute. Serve over a bed of your favorite staple. Serves 4.

TAHINI SAUCE

2 tbsp. (30 gm.) sesame seeds
½ tsp. (2 ml.) sesame oil
¼ tsp. (1 gm.) salt
¼ cup (60 ml.) warm water

Put sesame seeds in a blender and grind until smooth. Add the oil and salt and blend for 30 seconds. Slowly pour in the warm water and process until smooth. Makes ½ cup (125 ml.).

TWICE-COOKED RICE

Create your own version of this recipe with different vegetables

    2 tbsp. (30 ml.) canola oil
    2 eggs
    1 tbsp. (15 ml.) sesame oil
    3 cups (675 gm.) cooked rice, chilled
    1 clove garlic, minced
    1 cup (225 gm.) broccoli, cut into small florets
    1 cup (225 gm.) carrots, sliced thin
    1 can (8 oz. [225 gm.]) corn kernels, water drained
    2 stalks green onions, sliced
    2 tbsp. (30 ml.) soy sauce
    ½ tsp. (2 gm.) cayenne pepper

Heat just 1 tbsp. (15 ml.) of the canola oil in a wok or large, nonstick skillet. Beat the eggs with a fork or whisk for 30 seconds. Add the eggs to the skillet and stir until just set. Remove the eggs and set aside.

Heat the remaining canola oil and sesame oil. Add the rice and vegetables and stir-fry for 5-6 minutes.

Add the soy sauce, pepper, and cooked eggs. Stir-fry approximately 2 minutes. Serves 5-6. Serve hot. Leftovers can be served cold (pack in a container for lunch).

Variations: Use green beans, water chestnuts, celery, or frozen mixed vegetables in different combinations with either the broccoli, carrots, or corn.

Hint: The rice must be chilled, so several days before preparing Twice-Cooked Rice, prepare a rice meal with an extra amount of rice.

VEGETABLE AND RICE CASSEROLE

The blend of vegetables, rice, and pine nuts is enticing.

2 tbsp. (30 ml.) canola oil
1 onion, chopped
2 celery stalks, chopped
1 carrot, chopped
8-10 oil-marinated sun-dried tomatoes, quartered
2 cups (450 gm.) brown rice
4 cups (1 l.) vegetable broth
1 tsp. (4 gm.) oregano
1 cup (115 gm.) pine nuts

Preheat the oven to 400 degrees (204 degrees Celsius).

Heat the oil in a skillet over medium-high heat. Add the onion, celery, and carrot and sauté for 4-5 minutes. In a lightly greased 2-quart (2-l.) casserole dish, add the sautéed vegetables, tomatoes, rice, broth, and oregano and stir to mix. Cover tightly with a lid or foil and bake 40-45 minutes in the preheated oven. Remove the casserole, uncover, and sprinkle with pine nuts. Return to the oven and bake 8 minutes. Serves 6-8.

BROWN RICE AND SPINACH

This recipe has all the ingredients to make it a favorite meal.

1 tbsp. (15 ml.) canola oil
1 onion, chopped
2 cups (500 ml.) water
1 vegetable bouillon cube
1 cup (225 gm.) long-grain brown rice
1 pkg. (10 oz. [285 gm.]) fresh, washed spinach
½ tsp. nutmeg
½ cup (115 gm.) nuts (cashews or walnuts)

Heat oil in a large saucepan over medium heat. Add the onion and sauté until tender. Add the water and bouillon and bring to a boil. Stir in rice, cover, reduce heat to low, and simmer for 45 minutes. Stir in the spinach and nutmeg and cook 2-3 minutes. Let stand, covered, for 5 minutes. Stir in nuts and serve. Serves 4.

BLACK-EYED PEAS IN SPICY SAUCE

Serve over boiled or microwave-cooked potatoes or cooked pasta.

¼ cup (60 ml.) canola oil
1 onion, chopped
2 cloves garlic, minced
2 large tomatoes, chopped
2 tsp. (8 gm.) garam masala
2 tbsp. (30 gm.) salsa
1 tbsp. (15 ml.) soy sauce
2 cans (15-16 oz. [425-450 gm.]) black-eyed peas

Heat the oil in a large skillet over medium-high heat. Add the onion, garlic, and tomatoes and stir-fry for 4-5 minutes. Stir in the garam masala, salsa, and soy sauce and cook for 2 minutes. Add the black-eyed peas, stir, and bring to a boil. Lower the heat and simmer for 15 minutes. Serves 4-6.

APPLE-RED KIDNEY BEAN RICE

This is the perfect vegetarian dish to serve during the holidays.

1 cup (250 ml.) apple cider
1 vegetable bouillon cube
2 stalks celery, chopped
1 onion, finely chopped
2 apples, unpared and finely diced by hand
   or in a food processor
¼ cup (60 gm.) raisins
1 tsp. (4 gm.) curry powder
½ tsp. (2 gm.) garam masala
2 cups (450 gm.) cooked leftover rice (or cooked Kashi)
1 can (15-16 oz. [425-450 gm.]) red kidney beans, drained

In a large saucepan, add the cider, dissolve the bouillon cube, and add the cider, celery, and onion; heat to boiling. Cover, reduce heat, and simmer for 5 minutes. Add the remaining ingredients; stir to mix. Cover and cook for 10-12 minutes. Serves 4-6.

VEGAN CHILI

Spicy and hearty for winter nights

¼ cup (60 ml.) canola oil
2 red bell peppers, diced
1 onion, chopped
2 zucchini, chopped
2 cans (16 oz. [450 gm.]) red kidney beans
1 can (16 oz. [500 ml.]) tomato sauce
1 cup (225 gm.) salsa
1 tbsp. (15 gm.) chili powder
1 tsp. (4 gm.) cumin power
1 tsp. (4 gm.) salt
½ tsp. (2 gm.) pepper

Heat the oil in a large, heavy skillet on medium-high heat, add the vegetables, and sauté for 5 minutes. Add the kidney beans, tomato sauce, salsa, and spices. Bring the chili to a boil, then lower the heat and simmer for 20 minutes. Serve over rice. Serves 8.

Tip: For texture, add prepared TVP® (see recipe), or crumble 8 Walnut Balls (see recipe) and add to the chili the final 5 minutes of simmering.

LISA'S BAKED POTATOES

Lisa, Vegetarians in the Fast Lane's *illustrator, is also a great cook!*
This is from her family's recipe collection.

BAKED POTATOES

4 large white baking potatoes, skin scrubbed

Preheat the oven to 400 degrees (204 degrees Celsius).

Bake the potatoes for 1 hour in the preheated oven. Cut each potato in half, remove the pulp, and mash up. Set the potato shells aside.

SPINACH-CHEESE POTATO FILLING

1 tbsp. (15 ml.) olive oil
2-3 cloves of garlic, pressed
½ onion, diced
2 tbsp. (30 ml.) red cooking wine
2 cups (450 gm.) shredded fresh spinach
½ cup (115 gm.) Parmesan cheese
½ cup (115 gm.) feta cheese, crumbled
1 cup (225 gm.) nonfat cottage cheese
1 cup (225 gm.) ricotta cheese
2 tsp. (8 gm.) dried basil

While the potatoes are baking, heat the olive oil in a large skillet and sauté the garlic and onions for 30 seconds. Add the cooking wine and sauté another 10-15 seconds. Add the spinach and sauté for 1 minute. Remove from the heat and place the spinach mixture into a large mixing bowl. Add all of the cheeses and the basil to the spinach mixture. Stir to blend. Add the spinach-cheese mixture to the potato pulp, stir to mix, and spoon back into the potato shells. Return to the oven and bake at 375 degrees (190 degrees Celsius) for 10-15 minutes. Serves 4.

MICROWAVE BAKED POTATOES

An all-in-one fast and flavorful meal

1 large white baking potato, skin scrubbed
¼ cup (60 gm.) nonfat yogurt
4 broccoli florets, precooked*
Dash paprika

Pierce the potato and place the potato on a microwave grill or paper towel. Cook on high power in the microwave oven for 12 minutes. Remove the cooked potato and slice approximately a ½-inch (1.25-cm.) horizontal strip off the top. Scoop out the center and place in a small mixing bowl. Mash the potato pulp with the backside of a fork. Add the yogurt and broccoli and mix together.

Spoon the potato mixture back into the potato shell. Cook on high power for 2 minutes. Sprinkle with paprika. Serves 1; prepare additional potatoes as needed for individual servings.

*Use leftovers or cook frozen broccoli in the microwave according to package instructions.

BAKED SWEET POTATO AND MOLASSES

Sweet potatoes have high amounts of vitamins A and C,
calcium, and iron, yet nutritionally appease a sweet tooth.

1 large sweet potato, skin scrubbed
1 tbsp. (15 ml.) molasses
1 tbsp. (15 gm.) sliced almonds

Pierce the potato and place on a microwave grill or paper towel. Cook on high power in the microwave oven for 12 minutes. Remove the baked sweet potato and slice open with a cut both horizontally and across the width of the potato, keeping the bottom of potato intact. Place the sweet potato in a microwave-safe bowl. With the backside of a fork, mash the sweet potato pulp. Spoon the molasses over the potato and mash into the pulp. Sprinkle on the almonds. Return to the microwave oven and cook on high for 1 minute. Serves 1.

SCALLOPED POTATOES AND BROCCOLI

Broccoli, a member of the Brassica family, has double the vitamin C of
orange juice, lots of beta carotene, and fiber. Eating broccoli, like other Brassica
vegetables—Brussel sprouts, cauliflower, collards, kale, cabbage, and turnips—
greatly reduces the risk of breast and colon cancer.

3 tbsp. (45 gm.) butter or canola margarine
4 medium potatoes, scrubbed and sliced thin
1 onion, chopped
½ tsp. (2 gm.) seasoned salt, like Lawry's®
2 pkgs. (10 oz. [285 gm.]) frozen chopped broccoli, thawed
1 can (10-11 oz. [285-310 gm.]) cheddar cheese soup
½ cup (125 ml.) milk
1 tsp. (4 gm.) paprika
½ tsp. (2 gm.) pepper

Heat the butter in a large skillet over medium heat. Add the potatoes and onion, sprinkle with seasoned salt, and sauté for 5 minutes. Add the broccoli and sauté for 2-3 minutes. In a small bowl, combine the soup, milk, paprika, and pepper. Pour the soup mixture over the vegetables, bring to a bubbly boil, reduce heat, cover, and cook for 20-25 minutes. Serves 4.

BROCCOLI-CREAM CORN BAKE

Be careful—this recipe is addictive!

1 pkg. (10 oz. [285 gm.]) frozen broccoli, thawed
1 can (14-15 oz. [400-425 gm.]) cream-style corn
6 mushrooms, sliced (optional)
¼ onion, chopped
1½ cups (340 gm.) cooked staple (bulgur, rice, or kasha)
1 egg, beaten
½ tsp. (2 gm.) paprika
½ tsp. (2 gm.) salt
2 tbsp. (30 gm.) Parmesan cheese, grated

Preheat the oven to 350 degrees (177 degrees Celsius).

In a lightly greased casserole dish, combine all of the ingredients, except the Parmesan cheese. Sprinkle the Parmesan cheese over the top of the casserole. Bake for 45 minutes in the preheated oven. Serves 4.

GREEN BEAN CASSEROLE

*This recipe utilizes modern-day prepared food ingredients
for busy life-styles—serves a basketball team!*

¼ cup (60 ml.) canola oil
1 onion, chopped
1 pkg. (2 lb. [900 gm.]) frozen hash brown potatoes
1 pkg. (16 oz. [450 gm.]) frozen green beans
1 can (8 oz. [225 gm.]) mushrooms, drained
1 can (6 oz. [170 gm.]) black olives, drained
2 tbsp. (30 ml.) Worcestershire sauce
¼ tsp. (1 gm.) cayenne pepper
1 cup (115 gm.) Monterey Jack cheese, grated

Heat the oil in a large skillet, add the onions and potatoes, and cook as directed on the package. Cook the frozen green beans in the microwave, as directed on the package, and drain well. Spread the cooked potatoes and onions in the bottom of a 4-quart (3.75-l.) microwave baking dish. Spoon the green beans, mushrooms, black olives, and Worcestershire sauce over the potatoes and onions. Sprinkle the cayenne pepper and cheese over the dish. Place the baking dish in the microwave and cook on high power for 2 minutes. Serves 10.

STUFFED BELL PEPPERS

This recipes minimizes clean up.

2 tbsp. (30 ml.) olive oil
1 large onion, chopped
2 cloves garlic, minced
l pkg. (14-16 oz. [400-450 gm.]) frozen tofu, thawed, rinsed, squeezed dry, and crumbled
1 cup (225 gm.) cooked rice or favorite staple—millet, kasha, barley, etc.
2 cups (450 gm./500 ml.) Marinara Sauce*
4 large bell peppers, stemmed and seeded
¾ cup boiling water
¼ cup (60 gm.) Parmesan cheese, grated

Preheat the oven to 350 degrees (177 degrees Celsius).

In a large saucepan, sauté the onion and garlic in hot oil for 4-5 minutes. Add the tofu, rice, and marinara sauce. Stir and cook for 4-5 minutes. Spoon the mixture into the bell peppers. Place the stuffed peppers upright in a baking dish and pour in the boiling water. Sprinkle cheese on top of the peppers. Bake for 1 hour in the preheated oven. Serves 4.

*There are several brands, like Classico® (no preservatives and delicious!), that can be substituted for the Marinara Sauce.

SHORT-ORDER STUFFED BELL PEPPERS

If using leftover millet or rice, this recipe takes only
10 minutes to prepare and cook in the microwave.

2 green bell peppers, cut in half lengthwise, stemmed, and
  seeded
¼ cup (60 ml.) water
2 cups (450 gm.) cooked millet or rice
½ cup (115 gm.) corn kernels
¾ cup (170 gm.) salsa
2 tbsp. (30 ml.) ketchup
Topping (optional): Favorite grated or sliced cheese, bread
  crumbs, or wheat germ

Place the bell peppers, hollow side up, in a microwave-safe casserole dish. Pour the water into the dish, cover, and cook in the microwave oven on high power for 5 minutes. While the peppers are cooking, mix the remaining ingredients, except the topping. Spoon the mixture into the pepper halves. Add the topping, if desired. Cover and cook on high for 3 more minutes. Serves 4.

VEGETABLE MEDLEY

Combining frozen vegetables and a cream soup base is a ten-minute meal.
For large appetites, serve over a favorite staple or toast.

1 can (10 oz. [285 gm.]) cream of celery soup
½ cup (125 ml.) milk
1 pkg. (16 oz. [450 gm.]) frozen mixed vegetables
½ tsp. (2 gm.) onion powder
½ cup (60 gm.) blanched almonds

In a small bowl, mix together the soup and milk. Put the vegetables in a 2-quart (2 l.) microwave-safe casserole dish. Add the onion powder to the soup mixture and mix together; lightly stir into the vegetables. Microwave on high for 10 minutes. Add the almonds and toss. Serves 4.

Variations: For variety try other cream soups like broccoli, mushroom, cheddar cheese, etc.

PARCHMENT PAPER VEGETABLES

Parchment paper can be located in natural food stores.

1 zucchini, cut into ½-by-3-inch (1.25-by-7.5-cm.) strips
15 asparagus tips
¼ cup (60 gm.) onions, finely chopped
1 portabella mushroom, finely cut into strips*
1 small carrot, cut into thin, 3-inch (7.5-cm.) strips
¼ cup (60 gm.) broccoli
1 shot of dry vermouth
2 tbsp. (30 ml.) olive oil
Dash salt
Dash pepper
24 inches of parchment paper

Preheat the oven to 350 degrees (177 degrees Celsius).

Fold the parchment paper in half, lengthwise. Place all of the vegetables on the paper, off-center of the fold. Pour the olive oil and vermouth evenly over the vegetables. Sprinkle the salt and pepper over the vegetables. Fold the parchment paper over the vegetables, tucking in an edge of approximately ¼ inch (.65 cm.) to enclose and seal the vegetables. Bake 15 minutes in the preheated oven. To serve, slice the center of parchment paper open and remove the vegetables. Serves 2-3.

*Button or Italian Brown varieties may be substituted.

ROSEMARY POTATOES

Rosemary makes potatoes taste better than ever.

¼ cup (60 ml.) olive oil
3 tbsp. (45 ml.) white wine
1 pkg. (16 oz. [450 gm.]) frozen potatoes
   or country fries, thawed
1 red pepper, chopped
½ tsp. (2 gm.) rosemary
½ tsp. (2 gm.) salt
½ tsp. (2 gm.) black pepper

While heating the oil in a large skillet over medium-high heat, mix the wine with the potatoes and red pepper. After the oil is hot, add the wine-coated potatoes and pepper. Lower the heat to medium and stir occasionally for 12-15 minutes. After the potatoes are cooked, sprinkle on the rosemary, salt, and pepper. Serves 4.

HOT SPINACH AND WALNUTS

Easy to prepare and high in folic acid, vitamins, and minerals

2 tbsp. (30 ml.) soy sauce
1 tbsp. (15 ml.) lemon juice
1 tsp. (4 gm.) minced garlic
2 tbsp. (30 ml.) walnut or peanut oil
2 lbs. (900 gm.) spinach (leaves and stems),
   rinsed and patted dry
½ cup (60 gm.) walnuts
½ tsp. (2 gm.) pepper

In a jar add the soy sauce, lemon juice, and garlic and shake briskly to mix.

In a wok or large skillet, heat the oil on high. Add the spinach and gently stir for 1 minute. Remove from heat. Add the sauce mixture, walnuts, and pepper. Toss lightly. Serves 4-5.

BAKED EGGPLANT PARMESAN

*Eggplant was originally cultivated in tropical Asia,
later becoming popular in the Mediterranean cultures.*

¼ cup (60 ml.) water
2 tsp. (8 gm.) sugar
1 cup (225 gm.) bread crumbs
1 eggplant (unpeeled), cut into ¼-inch (.65-cm.) slices
2 cups (450 gm.) Marinara Sauce
1 lb. (450 gm.) Mozzarella cheese, grated
½ cup (115 gm.) Parmesan cheese, grated

Preheat the oven to 350 degrees (177 degrees Celsius).

In a bowl, mix the water and sugar. Put the bread crumbs in a second bowl. Dip each eggplant slice first into the water mixture, then in the bread crumbs. In an 8-inch-square casserole dish, layer the ingredients: one cup of Marinara Sauce; half of the breaded eggplant, half of the Mozzarella cheese. Repeat the second layer in the same order. Spread the Parmesan cheese evenly over the top. Cover with a lid or aluminum foil; bake for 20 minutes in the preheated oven. Remove the casserole from the oven, take the lid off, and place in the broiler. Broil 5-8 minutes; cheese will be light brown and bubbly. Serves 4.

RATATOUILLE

*The microwave oven makes this classic favorite
ready to serve in less than 30 minutes.*

1 eggplant
¼ cup (60 ml.) olive oil
2 tsp. (8 gm.) minced garlic
1 onion, sliced
3 zucchini, sliced
1 green bell pepper, cut into strips
1 can (16 oz. [450 gm.]) tomatoes
2 tsp. (8 gm.) Italian seasoning
1 tsp. (4 gm.) dried parsley
Grated Parmesan cheese (optional)

Pierce the eggplant well with a fork and place in a microwave-safe dish. Cook 8 minutes on high power. Set aside. In a 2½-inch (6.25-cm.) glass or ceramic casserole, mix the olive oil, garlic, and onion. Cover and cook 4 minutes on high. Peel the cooled eggplant and cut into approximately 1½-inch (4-cm.) cubes. Add the eggplant, zucchini, and green pepper to the casserole. Cover and cook 5 minutes. Add the tomatoes, seasoning, and parsley. Cook, uncovered 6-8 minutes on high power. If desired, sprinkle with Parmesan cheese. Serves 6-8.

CREOLE BLACK-EYED PEAS AND VEGETABLES

Add a slice of corn bread and you have a real "down-home" meal.

1 lb. (450 gm.) fresh green beans, stem ends trimmed*
2 medium white turnips, peeled and cut in large chunks
Water
2 tbsp. (30 gm.) butter
1 medium onion, chopped
1 can (14 oz. [400 gm.]) stewed tomatoes
1 tsp. (4 gm.) thyme
½ tsp. (2 gm.) salt
1 can (16 oz. [450 gm.]) black-eyed peas

In a 4- to 5-quart (3.75-4.75-l.) pan, cover green beans and turnips with water and bring to a boil. Reduce heat, cover, and simmer about 18 minutes.

While the vegetables are cooking, melt the butter in a large skillet, add the onion, and sauté 5-6 minutes, stirring frequently. Add the tomatoes, thyme, and salt. Stir to break up the tomatoes and mix the ingredients. Stir in the black-eyed peas.

Drain the cooked green beans and turnips and add to the skillet. Stir a few times, cover, and cook about 15 minutes over low heat. Serves 6.

*To speed up the preparation time, substitute 1 large pkg. (1 lb. [450 gm.]) frozen green beans.

VEGAN-RONI

Children and adults love macaroni.

2 tbsp. (30 ml.) olive oil
1 onion, chopped
2 carrots, chopped
2 stalks celery, chopped
1 can (4 oz. [115 gm.]) water chestnuts, drained
½ tsp. (2 gm.) oregano
½ tsp. (2 gm.) salt
¼ tsp. (1 gm.) pepper
1 can (16 oz. [450 gm.]) tomato sauce
1 pkg. (8 oz. [225 gm.]) small macaroni, cooked and drained
½ cup (115 gm.) bread crumbs

Preheat the oven to 350 degrees (177 degrees Celsius).

Heat the oil in a skillet; sauté the vegetables for 5 minutes on medium heat. Add the oregano, salt, and pepper to the sautéed vegetables. Add the tomato sauce, stir, and bring to a boil. Lower the heat and simmer for 15 minutes. Add the cooked macaroni to the vegetable-sauce mix and stir. Pour the mixture into a casserole dish. Sprinkle the bread crumbs over the vegetables. Bake for 30 minutes in the preheated oven. Serves 4.

BUTTER BEAN CASSEROLE

A subtle licorice flavor makes this unique blend flavorful and filling.

1 can (15 oz. [425 gm.]) butter beans, drained
1 pkg. (24 oz. [680 gm.]) frozen potatoes (Potatoes O'Brien)
1 jar (4½ oz. [130 gm.]) sliced mushrooms, drained
¼ cup (60 gm.) wheat germ
1 tsp. (4 gm.) fennel seed

Preheat the oven to 400 degrees (204 degrees Celsius).

Mix the beans, potatoes, mushrooms, wheat germ, and fennel seed in a 13-by-9-by-2-inch (32.5-by-22.5-by-5-cm.) baking pan.

SAUCE

¼ cup (60 gm.) butter
¼ cup (60 gm.) flour
1 cup (250 ml.) milk

In a skillet over medium heat, melt the butter. Stir in the flour until blended; add the milk and stir continuously until the sauce thickens. Pour the sauce over the butter bean mixture. Bake for 30 minutes in the preheated oven. For crispier potatoes, when you remove the baking pan from the oven, place it under the broiler for 3-4 minutes. Serves 6.

BAKED BEANS

Four beans baked in molasses sauce

¼ cup (60 ml.) oil
2 large onions, chopped
½ cup (125 ml.) ketchup
½ cup (115 gm.) brown sugar
¼ cup (60 ml.) molasses
1 tsp. (4 gm.) mustard
1 can (15-16 oz. [425-450 gm.]) kidney beans
1 can (15-16 oz. [425-450 gm.]) lima beans
1 can (15-16 oz. [425-450 gm.]) butter beans
1 can (15-16 oz. [425-450 gm.]) vegetarian navy beans

Preheat the oven to 350 degrees (177 degrees Celsius).

In heavy skillet sauté onions in hot oil. Add the ketchup, brown sugar, molasses, and mustard. Reduce the heat to low and simmer for 15-20 minutes.

While the sauce is simmering, mix the beans in a baking/casserole dish. Pour the cooked sauce over the beans. Bake 1 hour in the preheated oven. Serves 6-8.

Note: If preferred, use 1 cup (225 gm.) each of dry beans instead of canned. Add enough water to cover beans and soak them overnight in a crock pot. Drain the beans and return them to the crock pot, add the sauce ingredients, and cook on low for 8 hours.

CHAPTER 7
Soups and Salads

Soup and/or salad can be a complete meal for lunch or dinner, an appetizer, or a nutritional snack. The popularity of soup and salad has existed since the dawn of humankind and in times of economic prosperity or hardship. For a novice cook, preparing soups and salads is less intimidating and more culinary safe to serve to others.

VEGETABLE BROTH

A basic vegetable broth for other vegetarian recipes

3 qt. (3 l.) water
3 unpeeled potatoes, scrubbed and quartered
5 carrots, peeled and cut into large pieces
6 celery stalks with leaves, chopped
2 onions, peeled and quartered
¼ head cabbage
1 bay leaf
8-10 peppercorns
½ tsp. (2 gm.) salt
¼ tsp. (1 gm.) pepper

Place all of the ingredients in a large pot. Bring to a boil on high heat, reduce heat, cover, and simmer 1 hour. Strain liquid. Use the vegetables for another recipe like the Spicy Salsa Vegetable Soup recipe, which follows. Freeze portions of the broth for other recipes. Makes 3 quarts (3 l.).

Hint: It is easy to store extra vegetable stock. Simply pour stock into ice cube trays. Let freeze, then remove frozen cubes and place in a sturdy plastic bag and tightly seal. Return to the freezer. Frozen vegetable stock can be stored up to six months.

Note: If homemade vegetable broth is not available as needed for the preparation of other recipes, use vegetable bouillon cubes found in natural food and grocery stores.

SPICY SALSA VEGETABLE SOUP

It is ninety percent made after preparing the Vegetable Broth.

1 can (4 oz. [115 gm.]) tomato paste
3 cups (750 ml.) vegetable broth
1 cup (225 gm.) salsa
½ tsp. (2 gm.) oregano
¼ tsp. (1 gm.) ground cumin
Leftover vegetables from the Vegetable Broth recipe (slice and
chop the vegetables into smaller bite-sized pieces)

Bring the paste, broth, salsa, and spices to a boil. Lower the heat and simmer for 30 minutes. Add the vegetables and cook for 5 minutes until the vegetables are heated. Serves 4.

Variation: Add cooked rice, pasta, or beans at the same time the vegetables are added.

VEGETABLE SAUTE SOUP

There's nothing more delicious than homemade vegetable soup.

¼ cup (60 ml.) red wine or vegetable broth
1 onion, chopped
3 carrots, chopped
2 cups (450 gm.) broccoli florets
2 medium potatoes, scrubbed or peeled
and chopped into small pieces
½ head cabbage, shredded
2 tomatoes, chopped
1 qt. (1 l.) vegetable stock
6-8 peppercorns
2 tsp. (10 ml.) Worcestershire sauce

In a large skillet, heat the wine and add the onion and carrots. Sauté for 2 minutes. Add the broccoli, potatoes, and cabbage. Sauté 2-3 minutes. Add the tomatoes and sauté for another 2-3 minutes. In a large saucepan, stir over medium-high heat the vegetable stock, peppercorns, and Worcestershire sauce. Bring to a boil, lower heat, and add the sautéed vegetables. Simmer the soup for 30 minutes. Serves 3-4.

DRY-MIX VEGETABLE SOUP

For a quick fix, or when the the cupboard
and refrigerator are almost bare, it's always a good idea
to keep on hand packages of dry vegetable soup and dip mix.

1 pkg. (1-2 oz. [30-60 gm.]) dry vegetable soup and dip mix
4 cups (1 l.) water or quantity as directed on package
½ cup (115 gm.) cooked pasta,* rice, or favorite staple

Prepare the soup according to package directions. Add the pasta, rice, or a staple the final 5 minutes of cooking time. Serves 2-3.

*While the soup is simmering, uncooked pasta can be added to cook in the time required, i.e., macaroni requires 12 minutes of cooking time.

CREAM OF SPINACH SOUP

Hot or cold this soup satisfies the palate.

1 pkg. (10 oz. [285 gm.]) frozen creamed spinach, thawed
1 can (10-11 oz. [285-310 gm.]) cream of mushroom
   or cheddar cheese soup
1½ cups (375 ml.) milk
¼ cup (60 gm.) sour cream or plain yogurt
½ onion, chopped
1 tsp. (5 ml.) lemon juice
⅛ tsp. (.5 gm.) thyme
⅛ tsp. (.5 gm.) pepper

Place all of the ingredients in a blender or food processor and blend until smooth. Pour into a large saucepan and set the heat at medium-high. Bring the soup to a boil while stirring constantly. Turn off the heat and serve or chill in the refrigerator. Serves 3-4.

ORIENTAL SPINACH SOUP

Gingerroot and red pepper flakes add the sizzle to this spinach soup.

1 tsp. (5 ml.) sesame oil
1½ tbsp. (22 gm.) gingerroot, peeled and minced
1 clove garlic, minced
3 cups (750 ml.) homemade Vegetable Broth or substitute with
   2 cans (13-14 oz. [370-400 gm.]) vegetable broth
1 pkg. (10 oz. [285 gm.]) frozen chopped spinach
⅛ tsp. (.5 gm.) red pepper flakes
9-10 green onions, thinly sliced

In a medium-sized saucepan, heat the sesame oil on medium-high heat. Add the gingerroot and garlic and stir for 2 minutes. Add the vegetable broth, spinach, and red pepper flakes. Bring to a boil. Reduce the heat and simmer uncovered for 10 minutes; stir occasionally. Turn off the heat and add the green onions. Serves 3-4.

CORN AND SPINACH SOUP

Cooks in only 4 minutes

1 can (16 oz. [450 gm.]) whole corn kernels
¼ onion, chopped
1 garlic clove, minced
2 tbsp. (30 gm.) sugar
½ tsp. (2 gm.) salt
3 cups (750 ml.) vegetable broth
1 cup (225 gm.) fresh spinach, stems removed

In a medium saucepan, put all of the ingredients, except the spinach. Bring to a boil, reduce the heat, and simmer uncovered for 2 minutes. Add the spinach and cook for 2 minutes. Serves 2-3.

SWEET CORN AND CHILI PEPPERS

Serve with thick slices of squaw bread and a pasta salad

1 tbsp. (15 ml.) olive oil
1 pkg. (10 oz. [285 gm.]) frozen sweet corn, thawed
1 can (4 oz. [115 gm.]) green chilies, diced
1 tbsp. (15 gm.) minced garlic
4 cups (1 l.) vegetable stock
1 medium red potato, scrubbed and chopped
1 tsp. (4 gm.) cumin powder
¼ tsp. (1 gm.) cayenne pepper
Salt and pepper to taste
½ small red onion, diced fine
4 tsp. (16 gm.) dried cilantro or a few fresh sprigs chopped
2 limes, halved

In a large saucepan, heat the oil over medium heat; add the corn and stir for 5 minutes. Add the chilies and garlic and stir for 2 more minutes. Add the vegetable stock, potato, cumin, and cayenne; bring to a boil, turn the heat down to low, and simmer uncovered for 30 minutes. Season to taste with salt and pepper. Pour the soup into 4 bowls. Add 1 tbsp. (15 gm.) of onion and 1 tsp. (4 gm.) cilantro to each bowl. Squeeze approximately half a lime into each bowl and serve. Serves 4.

CURRY PEA SOUP

A soup from India—creamy with an exotic flavor

1 can (15-16 oz. [425-450 gm.]) peas, drained (reserve liquid)
3 cups (750 ml.) vegetable broth
2 tsp. (8 gm.) curry powder
1 tbsp. (15 gm.) sugar
¼ cup (60 gm.) flour and ⅓ cup (90 gm.) cold flour stirred
   together until lumpfree
¼ cup (60 gm.) slivered almonds
¼ cup (60 gm.) raisins
½ cup (115 gm.) light cream or yogurt
Salt and pepper to taste

Place the drained peas in a blender or food processor. Process on blend until smooth. In a medium-sized saucepan, add the processed peas to the vegetable broth, curry powder, sugar, and flour paste. Bring to a boil, stirring constantly. Add the almonds and raisins. Reduce the heat and simmer for 5 minutes. Remove the pan from the burner and add the cream. Season with salt and pepper. Serves 4-5.

BROCCOLI AND POTATO SOUP

Using frozen vegetables greatly reduces the preparation time.

1 tbsp. (15 ml.) olive oil
3 cloves garlic, minced
2 medium onions, chopped
¼ tsp. (1 gm.) dried sage
2 cups (450 gm.) water
6 cups (1.5 l.) vegetable broth
½ tsp. (2 gm.) salt
1 can (16 oz. [450 gm.]) whole potatoes, sliced
1 pkg. (10 oz. [285 gm.]) frozen broccoli
⅔ cup (180 gm.) plain yogurt
Few drops hot pepper sauce
Pinch black pepper

Heat the oil in 3-quart pot over medium-high heat. Add the garlic, onions, and sage. Cook until the onions are tender, about 5 minutes, stirring frequently. Add the water, vegetable broth, salt, potatoes, and broccoli. Cook, covered, about 8 minutes. Strain the vegetables, reserving the liquid. Purée the vegetables in a blender or food processor until smooth. Add ¼ cup (60 ml.) of the broth and the yogurt; blend until smooth.

Combine the puréed mixture and the remaining soup broth in the pot and add the pepper sauce and black pepper. Cook and stir 1 minute. Serves 6.

BROCCOLI SOUP

The tarragon herb makes this soup licorice-sweet.

4 cups (900 gm.) broccoli florets
2 cups (500 ml.) vegetable broth
1 small onion, chopped
½ tsp. (2 gm.) dried tarragon, crumbled

Place all of the ingredients in a medium saucepan; stir to mix. Over medium-high heat, bring to a boil. Reduce the heat to medium, cover, and cook 5 minutes until the broccoli is tender but still bright green. Place the mixture in food processor or blender, cover, and purée until smooth. Cover and refrigerate 2 hours before serving. Serves 4.

MULLIGATAWNY

Sweet and spicy flavors from India

2 tsp. (10 ml.) canola oil
1 large onion, chopped
1 zucchini, chopped
1 tsp. (4 gm.) tumeric
1 tsp. (4 gm.) cumin powder
¼ tsp. (1 gm.) cayenne pepper
2 tsp. (8 gm.) coriander powder
4 cups (1 l.) water or vegetable broth
1 large potato, scrubbed clean and cut into small cubes
1 carrot, chopped
1 large tomato, chopped
1 red pepper, seeded and chopped
1 cup (250 ml.) coconut milk
½ cup (125 ml.) unsweetened grated coconut
Juice of ½ lemon
Garam masala (optional)

Heat the oil in a large saucepan; sauté the onions and zucchini until translucent, about 5 minutes. Add the tumeric, cumin, cayenne, and coriander; stir for 1 minute. Add the water, potatoes, and carrots; bring to a boil. Cover, reduce heat, and simmer for 10 minutes. Add the tomato, pepper, coconut milk, and grated coconut; simmer for 8-10 minutes. Stir in the lemon juice; simmer for 1 minute. Sprinkle with garam masala for an extra dash of spice. Serves 5-6.

DAL SOUP

A favorite dish in Calcutta. Indian lentils (dal) are larger than Mediterranean varieties. While lentil beans do not require overnight soaking, Indian recipes using dal-lentils are soaked overnight so the lentils are mushier for a thicker soup.

1½ cups (340 gm.) lentil beans
Water to cover
4 cups (1 l.) water
¼ tsp. (1 gm.) tumeric
Dash salt
2 tbsp. (30 ml.) olive oil
½ tsp. (2 gm.) cumin seeds
1 cup (225 gm.) chopped onions
1 garlic clove, minced
2 tbsp. (30 ml.) orange or lemon juice
1 tsp. (4 gm.) garam masala or allspice

Rinse the lentil beans. Cover the lentils with water and soak overnight. Drain, add the 4 cups of water, tumeric, and salt. Bring to a boil, reduce heat, and simmer 30-40 minutes, stirring a few times.

In a cast-iron skillet, heat the oil, add the cumin seeds, and stir for 15-20 seconds. Add the onion and garlic; sauté 8-10 minutes. Add this mixture and remaining ingredients to the Dal Soup and cook 5 minutes. Serves 4-5.

LENTILS AND COUSCOUS SOUP

A healthy blend of proteins and fiber

8 cups (2 l.) vegetable broth
1 cup (225 gm.) uncooked lentils
1 bay leaf
3 garlic cloves, minced
1 tbsp. (15 gm.) minced onion
1 tsp. (4 gm.) cumin
1 tsp. (4 gm.) garam masala
½ cup (115 gm.) couscous
1 tbsp. (15 ml.) lemon juice

In a large, heavy saucepan, bring the first seven ingredients to a boil over high heat. Reduce the heat to low, partially cover, and simmer for 1½-2 hours. Add the couscous and lemon juice. Cover and simmer 5 minutes, stirring occasionally. Serves 6-8.

PAPRIKA LENTIL SOUP

Paprika enhances this lentil soup.

2 tbsp. (30 ml.) canola oil
1 medium onion, chopped
2 garlic cloves, minced
2 carrots, diced
2 stalks celery, diced
1 tomato, chopped
1 cup (225 gm.) dried lentils
8 cups vegetable broth
1 tsp. (4 gm.) cumin seeds
1 tbsp. (15 gm.) paprika
Salt and pepper to taste

Heat the oil in a large saucepan on medium-high; sauté the vegetables in hot oil for a few minutes. Add the lentils and sauté for 5 minutes. Add the broth and spices; bring to a boil. Reduce the heat, cover, and simmer for 1 hour. Serves 8.

MUSHROOM BARLEY SOUP

This recipe first appeared in Souper Skinny Soups.
At book signings, we substituted vegetable broth for the beef broth
because so many vegetarians wanted to taste-test this recipe.

4 cups (1 l.) vegetable broth
2 onions, chopped
3 carrots, sliced
½ lb. (225 gm.) mushrooms, sliced (approximately 18-20
   medium-sized mushrooms)
½ cup (115 gm.) barley, rinsed and drained
¼ cup (60 gm.) fresh parsley or 2 tsp. (8 gm.) dried parlsey
   flakes
¼ tsp. (1 gm.) black pepper

Place all of the ingredients in a large, heavy saucepan. Bring to a boil over medium-high heat. Lower the heat and simmer, partially covered, for 60-70 minutes or until the barley is tender. Serve hot. Serves 4.

FOUR BEAN SOUP

You may never soak beans again after trying this soup!

1 can (15-16 oz. [425-450 gm.]) black beans, with reserve
1 can (15-16 oz. [425-450 gm.]) pinto beans, with reserve
1 can (15-16 oz. [425-450 gm.]) blackeye peas, with reserve
1 can (15-16 oz. [425-450 gm.]) great northern beans,
   with reserve
4 cups (1 l.) water
1 vegetable bouillon cube
1 onion, chopped
4 stalks celery, chopped
1 can (14-15 oz. [400-425 gm.]) stewed tomatoes
1 tsp. (4 gm.) cumin powder
1 tsp. (4 gm.) oregano
Salt and pepper to taste

In a large saucepan, add all of the ingredients. Stir and bring to a boil, reduce the heat, and simmer 25-30 minutes. Serves 6.

WALNUT BALL SOUP

Another Oriental culinary delight to eat and savor

1 recipe Walnut Balls
2 tsp. (8 gm.) fresh grated or minced ginger, or 1 tsp. (4 gm.)
dry ground ginger
5 cups (1.25 l.) vegetable stock
1 tsp. (4 gm.) soy sauce
½ tsp. (2 gm.) salt
3 carrots, sliced thick
½ pkg. (4 oz. [60 gm.]) vermicelli spaghetti (cook and drain
while preparing soup)

Add the ginger to the walnut ball recipe. Shape the mixture into tiny walnut balls. Set aside uncooked walnut balls.

In a saucepan add the stock, soy sauce, salt, and carrots. Bring to a boil. Drop the walnut balls into the boiling soup, reduce heat slightly, and boil gently for 15 minutes.

Divide the cooked vermicelli into 4 bowls; add the soup. Serves 4.

CREAM OF VEGETABLE SOUPS

A basic cream sauce and many choices of vegetables and seasonings
from a fresh vegetable and seasoning chart

1½ cups (375 ml.) vegetable broth
½ small onion, chopped
Choice of vegetable and seasoning(s) from chart
2 tbsp. (30 gm.) butter or margarine
2 tbsp. (30 gm.) all-purpose flour
½ tsp. (2 gm.) salt
Few dashes white pepper
1 cup (250 ml.) low-fat milk

CONVENTIONAL DIRECTIONS

In a saucepan combine the vegetable broth, onion, and your uncooked choice of a fresh vegetable and seasoning(s) combination. Bring the mixture to boiling. Reduce heat; cover and simmer the time indicated in the chart or until the vegetable is tender. Place half of the cooked vegetable mixture into a blender or food processor. Cover and blend 30-60 seconds or until smooth. Pour into a bowl. Repeat with the remaining vegetable mixture; set aside.

In the same saucepan, melt the margarine. Blend in the flour, salt, and pepper. Add the milk; cook and stir until the mixture is thick and bubbly. Stir in the vegetable mixture. Cook and stir until the soup is thoroughly heated.

MICROWAVE DIRECTIONS

In a microwave-safe bowl, combine the amount of water shown in the microwave section of the chart, onion, and your choice of a fresh vegetable and seasoning(s) combination. Microwave the vegetable mixture the time indicated in the chart. Add the vegetable broth to the cooked vegetable mixture.

Blend or process the cooked vegetable/seasoning combination and broth as above. Set aside. In a 1½- (1.5-l.) or 2-qt. (2-l.) casserole dish, microwave the margarine, uncovered, on high power 30-60 seconds until melted. Stir in the flour, salt, and pepper. Add the milk all at once. Cook uncovered on high for 3-5 minutes until bubbly and thick; stirring every minute until bubbly, every 30 seconds when thickened. Stir in the vegetable-broth mixture. Cook uncovered on high 3-5 minutes until heated through; stop and stir once. If too thick, add milk to the desired consistency.

FRESH VEGETABLE AND SEASONINGS CHART

VEGETABLE	SEASONINGS	CONVENTIONAL VEGETABLE COOKING TIME	MICROWAVE VEGETABLE COOKING TIME POWER: HIGH
3 cups (675 gm.) cut asparagus	1 tsp. (5 ml.) lemon juice $1/8$ tsp. (.5 gm.) ground mace or nutmeg	8 minutes	7-10 minutes in 2 tbsp. (30 ml.) water
2 cups (450 gm.) cut green beans	½ tsp. (2 gm.) dried savory, crushed	20-30 minutes	13-15 minutes in 2 tbsp. (30 ml.) water
2 cups (450 gm.) cut broccoli	½ tsp. (2 gm.) thyme, crushed 1 small bayleaf (remove after cooking) 1 dash garlic powder	10 minutes	4-7 minutes in 2 tbsp. (30 ml.) water
2 cups (450 gm.) sliced carrots	1 tbsp. (15 gm.) snipped parsley ½ tsp. (2 gm.) dried basil, crushed OR 1 dash nutmeg or mace	12 minutes	7-10 minutes in 2 tbsp. (30 ml.) water
3 cups (675 gm.) sliced cauliflower	½-¾ tsp.(2-3.5 gm.) curry powder	10 minutes	7-10 minutes in 3 tbsp. (45 ml.) water

VEGETABLE	SEASONINGS	CONVENTIONAL VEGETABLE COOKING TIME	MICROWAVE VEGETABLE COOKING TIME POWER: HIGH
2½ cups (565 gm.) chopped celery	2 tbsp. (30 gm.) snipped parsley ½ tsp. (2 gm.) dried basil, crushed OR ½ tsp. (2 gm.) dried dill	15 minutes	6-10 minutes
1 cup (225 gm.) sliced mushrooms	⅛ tsp. (.5 gm.) ground nutmeg	5 minutes	3-4 minutes in 2 tbsp. (30 gm.) diet margarine
3 medium potatoes, sliced	½ tsp. (2 gm.) dried basil, crushed (add a shot of vinegar after cooked)	10 minutes	6-8 minutes in 2 tbsp. (30 ml.) water
4 medium tomatoes, peeled, quartered, and seeded	¼ tsp. (1 gm.) dried basil, crushed ¼ tsp. (1 gm.) garlic	15 minutes	10-12 minutes in 2 tbsp. (30 ml.) water
2 cups (450 gm.) cut unpeeled zucchini	2 dashes ground nutmeg	5 minutes	4-5 minutes in 2 tbsp. (30 ml.) water
16 cups (3.6 kg) fresh spinach	⅛ tsp. (.5 gm.) nutmeg	3-5 minutes	7-9 minutes in 2 tbsp. (30 ml.) water

WALDORF SALAD

A classic salad for classy vegans

3 apples, cored and diced
1 cup (225 gm.) grapes
1 cup (225 gm.) celery, chopped
½ cup (60 gm.) walnuts, chopped
2 tbsp. (30 ml.) lemon juice
½ cup (115 gm.) mayonnaise
2 tbsp. (30 ml.) light cream or whole milk

In a large bowl, toss the fruits, celery, and nuts in lemon juice. Blend the mayonnaise and milk; add to the salad and mix. Refrigerate for several hours before serving. Serves 4.

Tip: For variation, add raisins, toasted pine nuts, or sunflower seeds.

LAYERED LETTUCE-PEA SALAD

A green salad prepared a day ahead

1 head lettuce, cleaned and cut into small bite-sized pieces
1 cup (225 gm.) celery, finely chopped
1 pkg. (10 oz. [285 gm.]) frozen peas, thawed
½ green pepper, diced
1 onion, finely chopped
2 cups mayonnaise
2 tbsp. (30 gm.) sugar
½ cup (115 gm.) cheddar cheese, grated (optional)

Layer the lettuce on the bottom of a 12-by-9-inch (30-by-22.5-cm.) glass or ceramic baking dish. Layer the remaining vegetables in the order given. Mix the mayonnaise and sugar; spread over the top of the salad. Top with cheese. Refrigerate for 8-10 hours. Serves 10-12.

Note: Because this salad is made with mayonnaise, it should be returned to the refrigerator within an hour after it is served if there is any left in the baking dish. The leftover salad should be eaten within 24 hours.

VEGETABLE COLE SLAW

Lots of vegetables for a tangy slaw

1 medium head cabbage, shredded
2 carrots, shredded
1 green pepper, diced
2 green onions, chopped
1 stalk celery

Combine the vegetables and toss.

SWEET AND SOUR DRESSING

1½ cups (340 gm.) sugar
1 cup (250 ml.) vinegar
½ tsp. (2 gm.) dry mustard
½ tsp. (2 gm.) salt
1 cup (250 ml.) canola oil
1 tsp. (4 gm.) celery seed

In a saucepan, bring the sugar, vinegar, mustard, and salt to a boil. Turn off the heat and let cool. Pour the oil into a blender and add the cooled sugar-vinegar mix and celery seed. Process for 1 minute. Pour half of the dressing over the Vegetable Cole Slaw and toss lightly. Refrigerate for several hours before serving. Serves 10.

Note: Reserve the remaining dressing for other salads.

GRANDPA HOWARD'S COLE SLAW

This is dedicated to Grandpa Howard, who often doubled this recipe and served it at his favorite charity functions or family gatherings.

1 medium head cabbage, shredded
½ cup (115 gm.) sugar
½ cup (125 ml.) white vinegar
1 cup (225 gm.) mayonnaise

Place the cabbage in a bowl. In a small bowl, mix together the sugar and vinegar; whisk until well blended. Add the mayonnaise and mix until well blended. Pour the dressing over the cabbage and toss well. Serves 8.

ORANGE AND RAISIN SLAW

Another twist to a healthful cabbage slaw recipe

¼ head of cabbage, thinly sliced
¼ cup (60 gm.) red onion, chopped
2 tbsp. (30 ml.) orange marmalade
2 tbsp. (30 ml.) balsamic vinegar
1 tbsp. (15 ml.) olive oil
¼ cup (60 gm.) raisins
¼ cup (60 gm.) walnuts, chopped
¼ tsp. (1 gm.) black pepper

Mix the cabbage and onion in a large salad bowl. Place the orange marmalade, vinegar, and olive oil in the blender; give a few whirls on blend. Pour the orange mixture over the cabbage and onion. Add the raisins and toss. Chill in the refrigerator a few hours before serving. Sprinkle walnuts and pepper on top when ready to serve. Serves 4.

JAPANESE CABBAGE SALAD

The blend of cabbage, pear, and mango—an exotic salad

2 cups (450 gm.) shredded cabbage
1 unpeeled ripe pear, cubed
1 fresh mango, cubed (use mandarian oranges when mangos
  are not available)
¼ cup (60 gm.) unsalted pumpkin seed kernels, toasted
¼ cup (60 ml.) rice vinegar or white vinegar
2 tbsp. (30 ml.) soy sauce
1 tbsp. (15 gm.) sugar
¼ tsp. (1 gm.) garlic powder
Dash salt

Divide the cabbage in four salad bowls. Spread ¼ cup (60 ml.) of the pear and mango cubes on each of the cabbage-lined salad bowls. Sprinkle 1 tbsp. (15 ml.) of the pumpkin seeds in each bowl. Combine the remaining ingredients in a small jar. Cover and shake vigorously. Drizzle an equal portion of the vinegar-soy sauce mix over each salad. Serves 4.

BEAN SPROUT SALAD

Vegetarians enjoy food from around the world—this salad is from Japan.

1 pkg. (8-10 oz. [225-285 gm.]) frozen petite peas
Water
2 cups (450 gm.) bean sprouts, rinsed in cold water and
    drained
3 green bell peppers, thinly sliced
1 tbsp. (15 ml.) soy sauce
1 tbsp. (15 ml.) canola oil
1 tsp. (5 ml.) sesame oil
1 tbsp. (15 gm.) toasted sesame seeds

In a medium saucepan, pour enough water to cover the peas. Bring to a boil, reduce heat, cover, and simmer 3 minutes. Add the bean sprouts and bell peppers. Turn off the heat, cover, and let stand 2 minutes. Place the vegetables in a colander and rinse under cold water. Let drain. In a glass or ceramic bowl, mix the soy sauce and oils. Add the vegetables and toss. Sprinkle with the toasted sesame seeds. Serves 4.

HOT POTATO SALAD

A variation on the traditional German potato salad

6-8 potatoes, skins scrubbed
2 tbsp. (30 ml.) canola oil
1 medium onion, chopped
2 tbsp. (30 gm.) flour
2 tbsp. (30 gm.) sugar
¼ cup (60 ml.) vinegar
¾ cup (180 ml.) water
1¼ tsp. (5 gm.) salt
¼ tsp. (1 gm.) pepper
1 can (2-3 oz. [60-90 gm.]) French-fried onion rings

Cover the potatoes in their jackets with water and bring to a boil on high heat. Lower the heat and cook 15-20 minutes. Peel the potatoes and slice thinly. In a skillet heat the oil. Add the onion and sauté for 5 minutes. Stir in the flour and blend. Add the sugar, vinegar, water, salt, and pepper. Bring to a boil, stirring constantly until bubbly and thick. Remove from heat. Pour over the cooked and sliced potatoes. Stir to mix. Crumble the onion rings on top and serve immediately. Serves 6.

COLD POTATO SALAD

A traditional favorite to enjoy at a picnic with a zillion ants!

10 potatoes, skins scrubbed
Water
6 hard-boiled eggs, sliced
1 carrot, thinly chopped
4 stalks celery, chopped
4 stalks green onions, chopped
1 onion, chopped
5-6 mushrooms, chopped
2 cups (450 gm.) mayonnaise
¼ cup (60 gm.) relish
2 tbsp. (30 ml.) prepared mustard
1 tsp. (4 gm.) celery seed
Salt and pepper to taste
½ tsp. (2 gm.) paprika

In a large pot, cover potatoes with water and bring to a boil. Lower the heat and cook 15-20 minutes. Drain the water and let the potatoes cool. Peel the potatoes and dice in large pieces. In a large bowl, place the potatoes, eggs, carrot, celery, green onions, onion, and mushrooms. In a small bowl, mix the mayonnaise, relish, mustard, celery seed, salt, and pepper; gently fold into the eggs and vegetables. Sprinkle with paprika. Serves 10-12.

TOFU SALAD

Vinegar adds zip to tofu for a salad or sandwich spread.

1 pkg. (14-16 oz. [400-450 gm.]) tofu, crumbled
1 stalk celery, chopped
¼ onion, chopped
2 tsp. (10 ml.) apple cider vinegar
2 tsp. (10 ml.) honey
3 tsp. (12 gm.) prepared mustard
1 tsp. (4 gm.) tumeric
¼ tsp. (1 gm.) paprika

In a medium bowl, add the tofu, celery, and onion. Put the vinegar, honey, mustard, tumeric, and paprika into a blender and blend thoroughly. Pour over the tofu and vegetables. Toss to mix. Serves 4.

SPINACH SALAD

A good source for iron, vitamin A, and folic acid

1 bunch fresh spinach, cleaned and torn into bite-sized pieces
½ red onion, sliced thinly
1 jar (4 oz. [115 gm.]) marinated artichoke hearts, drained

Toss with your favorite oil-and-vinegar dressing or the Sweet and Sour Dressing in the Vegetable Cole Slaw recipe. Serves 4.

Variation: Add a ½ cup (115 gm.) of toasted sesame or sunflower seeds.

BLACK BEAN AND CORN SALAD

A colorful salad high in flavor and nutrients

1 can (15 oz. [425 gm.]) corn, drained
1 can (15 oz. [425 gm.]) black beans, drained
3 stalks celery, chopped
2 stalks green onion, chopped
2 cups (450 gm.) salsa
¼ cup (60 ml.) red-wine vinegar

In a large bowl, combine all of the ingredients and mix well. Cover and chill for several hours. Serve on a bed of lettuce or spinach leaves, or as a topping for burritos. Serves 8.

WILD RICE AND RED ONIONS SALAD

A crunchy rice salad to accompany the main entrée

2 tbsp. (30 ml.) olive oil
3 large red onions, chopped
½ cup (125 ml.) vegetable broth or water
3 tbsp. (45 ml.) red-wine vinegar
2 cups (450 gm.) wild rice, cooked

Heat the oil in a heavy skillet over medium heat and sauté the red onions. Cook for 5-6 minutes. Add the broth and vinegar; simmer 8-10 minutes. Add the cooked rice and stir to heat the rice. Serve hot or cold. Serves 4.

TABOULE-BROCCOLI SALAD

This salad can be a side dish or a complete lunch.

1 pkg. (5.25 oz. [149 gm.]) Taboule Wheat Salad Mix
1 cup (250 ml.) cold water
1 tbsp. (15 ml.) olive oil
1 cup (225 gm.) fresh broccoli, coarsely chopped
1 tomato, chopped
1 carrot, chopped
2 stalks green onion, chopped
¼ cup (60 gm.) walnuts, chopped
¼ cup (60 ml.) oil-free Italian salad dressing

In a large bowl, combine the wheat with the contents of the "spice sack." Stir in the water and olive oil. Let stand 30 minutes. Add the remaining ingredients and toss gently. Cover and chill 4-8 hours. Serve on a bed of lettuce. Serves 3-4.

CUCUMBER SALAD

Marinated cucumbers are a traditional Japanese favorite.

3 medium cucumbers
⅓ cup (80 ml.) white-rice vinegar
4 tsp. (16 gm.) sugar
1 tsp. (4 gm.) salt
1 tsp. (4 gm.) fresh gingerroot, finely chopped

Peel the cucumbers and cut them in half lengthwise. Cut out the seeds. Slice the cucumbers crosswise into thin slices. Mix together the vinegar, sugar, salt, and ginger. Pour the marinade sauce over the cucumber slices. Let chill 2-3 hours. Serves 5-6.

TORTELLINI-VEGETABLE SALAD

*This salad is just the the cool solution
for a light dinner on a hot summer's evening.*

1 pkg. (9 oz. [255 gm.]) cheese tortellini
1 zucchini, finely chopped
1 large tomato, finely chopped
1 jar (6 oz. [175 gm.]) artichoke hearts, drained
2 stalks green onions, chopped
½ cup (60 gm.) pine nuts
¼ cup (60 ml.) Italian dressing

Cook the tortellini according to package directions. Rinse under cold water and drain in a colander. Combine the drained tortellini and the remaining ingredients in a bowl and toss gently. Serves 5-6.

Variation: Use other fresh vegetables such as crookneck squash, cucumber, or broccoli florets.

CUCUMBER RAITA

An Indian dressing to serve over salads or as a pita bread topping

1 large cucumber, peeled and chopped
1 cup (225 gm.) yogurt
1 tsp. (4 gm.) dried mint
¼ tsp. (1 gm.) chili powder
¼ tsp. (1 gm.) ground cumin
Pinch salt and pepper

Mix all of the ingredients and chill for at least 2 hours.

CUCUMBER-MINT SALAD

Cool and refreshing for hot, muggy days

4 cucumbers, peeled and sliced
¼ cup (60 gm.) fresh mint
¼ cup (60 gm.) fresh parsley, chopped, or ½ tsp. (2 gm.) dried parsley
1 tbsp. (15 ml.) lemon or lime juice
¼ tsp. (1 gm.) salt
1 tbsp. (15 ml.) olive oil

Toss the cucumbers with the remaining ingredients. This keeps in the refrigerator for several days.

Variation: Add a favorite staple (rice, pasta, millet, etc.) and other vegetables to create a main entrée.

ROMAINE SALAD

Romaine lettuce is a good source of folic acid.

1 head romaine lettuce, torn into bite-sized pieces
1 large tomato, chopped, or 1 cup (225 gm.) cherry tomatoes
½ red onion, sliced
1 cucumber, diced
¼ cup (60 gm.) fresh parsley, finely chopped

Toss the ingredients with your favorite dressing. Serves 4-6.

Variation: Add crumbled feta cheese, olives, and/or green bell peppers.

MANDARIN-ORANGE GELATIN SALAD

Sweet and tangy to complement a spicy dish

2 pkgs. (3 oz. [85 gm.] each) orange-flavored gelatin
1 envelop unflavored gelatin
2 cups (500 ml.) boiling water
1 cup (250 ml.) cold water
1 tbsp. (15 ml.) brandy flavoring (optional)
1 can (12 oz. [340 gm.]) mandarin oranges, drained;
   reserve ½ cup (125 ml.) liquid
½ cup (115 gm.) coconut, shredded

Combine the orange-flavored and unflavored gelatins in a large bowl and stir to mix. Add the boiling water and stir until the gelatin is dissolved. Stir in the cold water, brandy flavoring, mandarin oranges with the reserved liquid, and coconut. Chill for 2-3 hours. Serves 6.

FRUIT SALAD FROM INDIA

Another vegetarian dish that makes being a vegetarian
much more exciting than living on a meat and potato diet!

2 tangerines, peeled and fruit sections separated
2 bananas, peeled and cut into medium-sized pieces
2 pears, cored and chopped (do not peel)
1 apple, cored and chopped (do not peel)
2 kiwi, peeled and chopped (optional)*
Juice of 1 lemon
1 tsp. (4 gm.) ground ginger
1 tsp. (4 gm.) garam masala
1 tsp. (4 gm.) salt
½ tsp. (2 gm.) ground black pepper

Place the prepared fruit in a bowl and sprinkle the lemon juice over all. Mix together all of the spices and sprinkle over the fruit. Toss to cover the fruit; refrigerate 2-3 hours before serving. Serves 4.

*You can substitute guavas or mangos in place of the kiwi.

ROQUEFORT DRESSING

No preservatives!

¼ lb. (115 gm.) Roquefort cheese, crumbled
¼ cup (115 gm.) plain yogurt
¼ cup (60 ml.) olive oil
2 tbsp. (30 ml.) lemon juice
¼ tsp. (1 gm.) paprika
¼ tsp. (1 gm.) salt
Pinch pepper

Combine all of the ingredients in a jar with a tightly covered lid. Shake vigorously to mix.

Note: This is the only separate recipe for a salad dressing in *Vegetarians in the Fast Lane* because there are so many good, preservative-free salad dressings, like Bernstein's®, available in supermarkets that it's unneccessary to prepare them from scratch.

CHAPTER 8
Snacks and Desserts

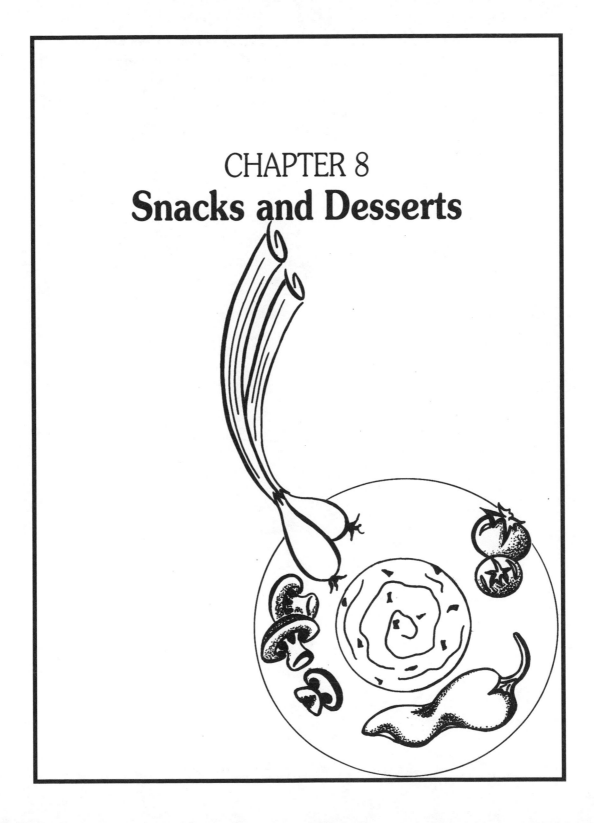

Waiting long periods of time between meals to eat is considered unhealthy. Snacks and desserts conjure up unhealthy food images, such as candy and potato chips. Actually, a snack can be a piece of fruit or slices of raw vegetables. Eating smaller portions of foods, 5 or 6 times a day, is much healthier than eating 3 large meals. Everyone needs a treat—enjoy this selection of snacks and desserts!

AVOCADO COUSCOUS SNACK

A snack prepared in just 8 minutes that provides over half of the required vitamin A and is loaded with amino acids, minerals, and other vitamins

½ cup (125 ml.) water
⅓ cup (90 gm.) couscous
¼ tsp. (1 gm.) salt
1 ripe avocado
½ tsp. (2 gm.) paprika or cayenne pepper

Bring the water to a boil. Add the couscous and turn the heat off. Cover the pan and let stand for five minutes. Meanwhile, slice the avocado the long way and remove the seed. Scrape a small amount of the avocado out around the seed hole. Fill the avocado with couscous and sprinkle with salt and the spice of your choice.

Note: There will be extra couscous, which can be stored in the refrigerator and reheated in a microwave oven. Serves 2.

Nutrition tip: Couscous is a healthy staple food from North Africa. While avocados are high in fat, the cholesterol count is zero. Unsaturated fat in a diet is healthy and important because unsaturated fats provide energy and act as carriers for the fat-soluble vitamins, A, D, E, and K.

SUNOMONO

Travis prepared this traditional Japanese dish as an appetizer for sushi patrons; for his version, he substitutes tofu for the crab and octopus.

2 cucumbers
Salt
3 tbsp. (45 gm.) sugar
2 tbsp. (30 ml.) rice vinegar
¾ cup (180 ml.) water
8 oz. (225 gm.) extra-firm tofu cut into ½-inch (2.5-cm.) cubes

Peel the cucumbers lengthwise with tiny strips of skin remaining. Cut them in half lengthwise and with the back of the peeler remove all of the seeds. Then cut horizontally in thin slices. Place the cucumbers in a small bowl and lightly salt them. In another small bowl, add the sugar, vinegar, and water; stir until the sugar is dissolved. Squeeze the excess water from cucumbers with a paper towel. Add the cucumbers and tofu to the vinegar-sugar mixture. Lightly toss and serve. Serves 3-4.

SPICY ROASTED WALNUTS

High protein food never tasted so good

3 tbsp. (45 ml.) olive oil
2 tsp. (8 gm.) dried rosemary, crushed
1 tsp. (4 gm.) sea salt
½ tsp. (4 gm.) cayenne pepper
2 cups (225 gm.) walnut halves

Preheat the oven to 350 degrees (177 degrees Celsius). Line a large baking sheet with foil.

In a small skillet heat the olive oil with the rosemary, salt, and cayenne. Turn off the heat and add the walnuts. Stir until the walnuts are coated evenly. Spread the coated nuts on the baking sheet. Roast in the preheated oven 12-15 minutes, stirring once or twice. Let cool and eat. Roasted walnuts can be wrapped in foil and stored up to 3 days at room temperature or a week in the refrigerator. Makes 2 cups (225 gm.).

Hint: Blanching walnuts removes the thin brown skin, which has a tannic taste—a dry, astringent aftertaste. For a buttery flavor, blanching might be preferred. To blanch, drop the shelled walnuts into briskly boiling water. Cook for two minutes at a rolling boil. Drain in a colander, rinsing well with cold water. Spread the walnuts on a paper towel and pat dry and eat, cook, or freeze.

NUTRITIONAL VALUE OF WALNUTS

A ¼ cup (60 gm.) has 130 calories, 4 grams of protein, and linolenic acid (an Omega-3 fatty acid essential to metabolism and aids in reducing blood-cholesterol levels).

ORANGE PECAN CANDY

A sweet treat to enjoy after a hard day's work

1 cup (225 gm.) sugar
¼ cup (60 ml.) orange juice
1 tbsp. (15 gm.) grated orange peel
¼ tsp. (1 gm.) ginger
4 cups (454 gm.) shelled pecan halves (approximately 1 lb.)

Line a cookie sheet with waxed paper. Bring the first 3 ingredients to a boil in a heavy, large saucepan. Cook over medium heat, stirring constantly. Boil 30 seconds. Stir in the ginger and pecan halves. Spread the pecans on the cookie sheet. Cool. Separate the pecans and store in an airtight container. Makes approximately 1 lb. (450 gm.).

Hint: Toasting pecans intensifies the flavor. Toast pecans in a single layer for 10 minutes in a 350-degree (177 degrees Celsius) oven, or 3-4 minutes in the microwave.

HOT PECANS

This snack can be frozen and ready to serve for unexpected guests.

1 lb. (450 gm.) shelled pecan halves
¼ cup (60 ml.) canola oil
⅓ cup (90 ml.) Worcestershire sauce
1 tsp. (4 gm.) Lawry's® seasoned salt or equivalent
8 dashes Tabasco® sauce, or equivalent

Preheat the oven to 350 degrees (177 degrees Celsius).

Place the pecan halves in a colander and rinse with steaming, hot water. Shake to drain and place the pecans on a paper towel. In a small bowl, whisk the oil, Worcestershire sauce, salt, and Tabasco®. Add the pecans and stir to coat. Remove the pecans and place on a foil-covered cookie sheet. Drip the remaining sauce over the pecans. Bake, stirring a few times, for 30 minutes in the preheated oven. Makes approximately 1 lb. (450 gm.). Double the recipe and freeze a portion to have ready at a moment's notice.

MEXICAN SALSA

Homemade salsa is easy to make—and less costly!

2 tbsp. (30 ml.) canola oil
½ onion, chopped
1 green chili, chopped
1 yellow chili, chopped
2 cans (15 oz. [425 gm.]) Mexican stewed tomatoes, undrained
1 tsp. (5 ml.) lime or lemon juice
1 tsp. (4 gm.) garlic powder
½ tsp. (2 gm.) chili powder
½ tsp. (1 gm.) cayenne pepper, optional
¼ cup (60 gm.) cilantro, cleaned and stems removed

Heat the oil in a small skillet. Add the onion and chilies; sauté for 2 minutes. Place the sautéed vegetables in a blender or processor. Add the tomatoes, lime juice, spices, and cilantro. Cover the blender and grate or chop for a few quick whirls. Manually stir and chop for another quick whirl. Pour into a glass container and store in the refrigerator. Makes more than 1 quart (1 liter).

Tip: Serve as a pasta or salad dressing, or baked potato topping. To reduce the chili pepper "heat," discard the seeds and omit the cayenne pepper. This will also make the salsa sweeter for a pasta or salad topping.

CRANBERRY SALSA

A holiday or party twist to salsa

1 can (16 oz. [450 gm.]) whole cranberry sauce
1 can (4 oz. [115 gm.]) diced green chilies, drained
1 tsp. (4 gm.) dried cilantro
¼ tsp. (1 gm.) ground cumin
1 green onion, chopped
1 tsp. (5 ml.) lime or lemon juice
2 tbsp. (30 gm.) pine nuts
½ tsp. (2 gm.) orange peel

Put all of the ingredients in a medium-sized bowl. Stir to mix. Refrigerate until ready to serve. Makes 2½ cups (625 ml.).

PINEAPPLE SALSA

Serve with tortilla chips or warm up and serve as a dip for the Walnut Balls.

1 can (20 oz. [565 gm.]) crushed pineapple, drained
1 can (4 oz. [115 gm.]) diced green chilies, drained
2 tsp. (8 gm.) cilantro, chopped
1 tsp. (5 ml.) lime juice

Combine all of the ingredients in a mixing bowl. Refrigerate until ready to serve. Makes 2 cups (500 ml.).

TOFU-ONION DIP

Tofu adds protein to a favorite dip.

8 oz. (225 gm.) tofu
1 cup (225 gm.) sour cream
1 pkg. (2-3 oz. [60-90 gm.]) onion soup mix

Mix all of the ingredients in the blender until smooth. Refrigerate for several hours before serving. Makes 2 cups (500 ml.).

SPINACH DIP

Serve with fresh vegetables and/or whole-wheat pita bread wedges.

1 pkg. (10 oz. [285 gm.]) frozen spinach, thawed, squeezed, and chopped
1 pkg. (8 oz. [225 gm.]) cream cheese, softened at room temperature
½ cup (115 gm.) plain yogurt or sour cream
1 carrot, shredded
1 stalk green onion, finely chopped
6½ tsp. (2 gm.) dried dillweed

In a microwave-safe casserole bowl, combine all of the ingredients. Cover with plastic wrap. Microwave on high power for 3-4 minutes, pausing and stirring several times during cooking. Serve warm. Makes 2 cups (500 ml.).

MUSHROOM-WALNUT PATE

Spread on wheat or rye crackers.

¼ cup (60 ml.) walnuts
¼ cup (60 ml.) red wine
1 vegetable bouillon
4 cups (900 gm.) mushrooms
¼ cup (60 gm.) plain yogurt or sour cream
½ tsp. (2 gm.) salt
¼ tsp. (1 gm.) dried parsley

In a blender or food processor, finely chop the walnuts. In a skillet on medium-high, heat the wine; add the bouillon and mushrooms. Stir and simmer for 5 minutes. Lower the heat, add the yogurt and parsley; stir just until blended. Add the mushroom-yogurt mixture to the walnuts in the blender; blend until smooth. Refrigerate until ready to serve. Makes 2 cups (500 ml.), serves 8-12.

MICROWAVE BAKED APPLES

A traditional favorite dessert prepared in minutes

1 cooking apple, washed and cored
1 tsp. (4 gm.) butter
1 tbsp. (15 ml.) maple syrup or molasses
2 tbsp. (30 gm.) walnuts
2 tbsp. (30 gm.) raisins
Pinch cinnamon
¼ cup (60 ml.) apple juice or water

Place the apple in a small microwave-safe bowl. Place the butter, maple syrup, and a few walnuts and raisins in the center of the apple. The remaining walnuts and raisins can be placed around the apple. Sprinkle on the cinnamon. Fill the bottom of the bowl with the juice. Microwave on high for 5 minutes. Let stand a few minutes before eating. Serves 1.

MICROWAVE APPLE CRISP

Another traditional favorite prepared in minutes

8-10 cooking apples, cleaned and sliced
½ cup (115 gm.) rolled oats
¼ cup (60 gm.) flour
¼ cup (60 gm.) brown sugar
⅛ tsp. (.5 gm.) nutmeg
½ tsp. (2 gm.) cinnamon
¼ cup (60 gm.) butter
1 tsp. (5 ml.) lemon juice

Place the sliced apples in an 8-inch (20-cm.) square microwave-safe baking dish. Mix the remaining ingredients and crumble over the top of the apples. Cover with waxed paper. Cook on high for 8-10 minutes. Serves 4-5. Top with whipped cream or vanilla ice cream.

LEFTOVER RICE PUDDING

Another delectable reason to always cook
extra amounts of rice for other recipes

1 tbsp. (15 ml.) butter
2½ cups (565 gm.) cooked white rice
1½ cups (340 gm.) evaporated milk
¼ cup (60 gm.) brown sugar
¼ cup (60 ml.) molasses
3 tbsp. (45 gm.) butter
2 tsp. (10 ml.) vanilla
½ tsp. (2 gm.) nutmeg
3 eggs, beaten
½ cup (115 gm.) raisins

Lightly grease with the 1 tablespoon of butter the inside of a crock pot or slow cooker. In a large bowl, stir the remaining ingredients together; pour into the crock pot. Cover and cook on high power for 1½-2 hours or low for 4-5 hours. Serves 4-6.

LEMON-TOFU BREAD PUDDING

Preparation time is easy and bakes in only 35-45 minutes

4 eggs
1 pkg. (14-16 oz. [400-450 gm.]) tofu
½ cup (125 ml.) honey
½ cup (125 ml.) molasses
½ cup (125 ml.) water
2 tbsp. (30 ml.) lemon juice
1 tsp. (4 mg.) lemon rind, grated
½ tsp. (2 ml.) vanilla
¼ tsp. (1 gm.) salt
2 cups dried bread cubes, ½-inch (1.25-cm.) squares

Preheat the oven to 350 degrees (177 degrees Celsius).

Blend all of the ingredients, except the bread cubes, in a blender until smooth. Pour the blended ingredients into a buttered 2-quart (2-l.) casserole. Add the bread cubes and gently stir. Bake 35-45 minutes in the preheated oven. Serves 4.

MOLASSES SNACK BARS

Good fast food for breakfast or snacks

½ cup (115 gm.) brown sugar
½ cup (125 ml.) molasses
½ cup (115 gm.) peanut butter
1 tsp. (5 ml.) vanilla
2½ cups (565 gm.) rice cereal
2 cups (450 gm.) rolled oats
½ cup (115 gm.) raisins
1 cup (225 gm.) walnuts or any kind of nuts

Place the brown sugar, molasses, and peanut butter in a large microwave-safe bowl. Microwave on high power for 2 minutes. Remove the bowl from the microwave and add the vanilla, stirring until blended. Add the rice cereal, oats, raisins, and walnuts and stir all of the ingredients until well blended. Press the mixture into a lightly buttered 13-by-9-inch (32.5-by-22.5-cm.) baking pan. After the mixture cools, cut into bars. Wrap the bars in plastic wrap and store in an airtight container. Makes 16 bars.

STOVETOP OATMEAL COOKIES

No baking—the perfect summer treat
to prepare without heating up the kitchen!

2 cups (450 gm.) sugar
¼ cup (60 gm.) margarine
⅓ cup (90 gm.) cocoa
½ cup (125 ml.) milk
2 cups (450 gm.) rolled oats
½ cup (115 gm.) chunky peanut butter
¼ cup (60 gm.) coconut (optional)

In a saucepan over medium heat, stir the sugar, margarine, cocoa, and milk for 2 minutes. Turn off the heat and add the oats, peanut butter, and coconut. Stir briskly to blend. Drop by spoonfuls on wax paper. Cool. Makes 28-30 cookies.

RICE AND FRUIT DESSERT

Another recipe using leftover cooked rice
for a "stir, eat, and go" treat

1 cup (225 gm.) cooked white rice
1 cup (225 gm.) fruit (canned or frozen),
   drained and/or thawed
¼ cup (60 gm.) walnuts, chopped
2 cups (500 gm.) whipped cream

Mix the rice, fruit, and walnuts together; fold in the whipped cream. Serve in dessert cups or dishes. Serves 4.

PUMPKIN DESSERT

Beta carotene, a vitamin A nutrient with antioxidant action
to fight diseases and aging is found in all orange/yellow vegetables.
This pumpkin dessert is made with evaporated skim milk
to reduce fat content for a healthful and flavorful treat.

1 cup (250 ml.) water
1 cup (250 ml.) apple cider
1 cup (225 gm.) kashi
1 can (29 oz. [825 gm.]) solid pumpkin
1 can (12 oz. [375 ml.]) evaporated skim milk
2 tsp. (8 gm.) pumpkin spice or allspice
1 tsp. (4 gm.) salt
2 eggs
¼ cup (60 ml.) molasses
1 cup (225 gm.) granulated sugar

Put the water and cider into a medium saucepan; bring to a boil. Add the kashi, reduce heat to medium-low, cover, and cook 25 minutes. In a large bowl, mix the pumpkin, milk, spices, eggs, molasses, and sugar until blended. Press the cooked kashi on the bottom and sides of a microwave-safe 9-inch (22- to 23-cm.) pie plate. Pour half* of the pumpkin mixture into the pie plate. Cook on high power for 15 minutes. Remove and let stand 15 minutes. Serves 6.

*Freeze the second half to cook at another time.

Variation: Eliminate the kashi pie crust and serve the pumpkin dessert in small dessert bowls or substitute the kashi pie crust with a ready-made pie crust or crumb crust.

Hint: Double the quantity of kashi, water, and apple cider. Store half of the cooked kashi-apple cider mixture in the refrigerator for another meal or reheat and serve for breakfast the next morning.

ITALIAN CASSATA

Dazzle your guests with a light dessert treat that's easy to prepare.

1 can (8 oz. [225 gm.]) crushed pineapple,
  juice drained and set aside
1 sponge cake loaf (8 oz. [225 gm.]),
  cut in half lengthwise through the center of the cake
1 cup (225 gm.) part-skim ricotta cheese
1 tbsp. (15 ml.) honey
1 tsp. (5 ml.) brandy, rum, or vanilla flavoring
¼ cup (60 gm.) miniature chocolate chips

Spoon the pineapple over the bottom layer of the sponge cake. Place the top layer of cake over the pineapple-spread layer. In the blender puree 3 tablespoons (45 ml.) of the pineapple juice, the ricotta cheese, honey, and brandy flavoring until smooth. Spread the ricotta cheese mixture over the top layer of sponge cake. Sprinkle with the chocolate chips. Cover and place in the refrigerator to chill 2-3 hours before serving. Serves 5-6.

Tip: Sponge cake is low in calories. It is a great base to use for quick-fix desserts like strawberry shortcake. And sponge cake can be served à la mode with melted chocolate drizzled over the top or with any favorite fruit topping.

GRANITAS

*The Italians created this "adult snowcone" dessert that starts
with a basic syrup and can be made with numerous fruit variations.*

BASIC GRANITA SYRUP

4½ cups (900 gm.) sugar
4 cups (1 l.) water

In a large saucepan, stir together the sugar and water. Bring mixture to a boil; cook 1 minute, stirring constantly. Makes 6 cups (1.5 l.).

BERRIES AND WINE GRANITA

4 cups (800 gm.) fresh or frozen and thawed berries (strawberry, blueberry, blackberry, rasberry)
2 cups (500 ml.) Basic Granita Syrup
2 cups (500 ml.) red wine

Place the berries in a food processor or blender. Process until smooth; pour into a large saucepan. Pour the Basic Granita Syrup and wine into the saucepan and bring to a boil. Reduce the heat and simmer, uncovered, for 3-4 minutes. Remove the saucepan from heat and let cool to room temperature. Pour the fruit mixture into an 8-inch (20-cm.) square glass or ceramic baking dish. Cover with plastic wrap and freeze for 8-10 hours. Remove from the freezer and scrape the mixture with the tines of a fork until fluffy. Spoon the granita into a container, cover, and return to the freezer until ready to serve. It stores in the freezer for up to a month. Makes 10 ½-cup (125 ml.) portions.

Hint: If a seedless, smooth granita is preferred, after processing the berries in the processor or blender, strain the fruit mixture through a sieve into the large saucepan. Remove the fruit solids from the strainer and save to use as ice-cream or yogurt topping.

ORANGE MARMALADE GRANITA

4 cups (1 l.) orange juice
1 cup (250 ml.) Basic Granita Syrup
2 tbsp. (30 gm.) orange marmalade
1 tbsp. (15 ml.) brandy (optional)

Put all of the ingredients in a food processor or blender and blend until smooth. Pour the mixture into a 13-by-9-by-2-inch (32.5-by-22.5-by-5-cm.) glass baking dish. Cover with plastic wrap and freeze 8-10 hours. Remove the orange mixture from the freezer and scrape the mixture with the tines of a fork until fluffy. Spoon the Orange Marmalade Granita into a container and cover and return to the freezer until ready to serve. Makes 14 ½-cup (125 ml.) portions.

LEMONADE GRANITA

4 cups (1 l.) lemonade
1 cup (250 ml.) Basic Granita Syrup
1 tbsp. (15 gm.) lemon zest

Put all of the ingredients in a food processor or blender and blend until smooth. Pour the mixture into a 13-by-9-by-2-inch (32.5-by-22.5-by-5-cm.) glass baking dish. Cover with plastic wrap and freeze 8-10 hours. Remove the lemonade mixture from the freezer and scrape the mixture with the tines of a fork until fluffy. Spoon the Lemonade Granita into a container and cover and return to the freezer until ready to serve. Makes 14 ½-cup (125 ml.) portions.

HERB TEA

Helps digest food

½ tsp. (2 gm.) dried peppermint leaves
½ tsp. (2 gm.) anise seeds
½ tsp. (2 gm.) caraway seeds
2 cups (500 ml.) water

Put the herbs in a tea ball. In a medium-sized pan, bring the water to a boil, lower the heat, and place the tea ball into the pan to steep for 5 minutes. This is a flavorful tea that is recommended for use after eating legumes. Serves 2.

Index